DATE DUE

101 THINGS
Parents
SHOULD Know
BEFORE
VOLUNTEERING TO

KAPCO

Teams

101 THINGS Parents SHOULD Know BEFORE VOLUNTEERING TO Coach THEIR KIDS' Sports Teams

DR. GARY S. GOODMAN

CB
CONTEMPORARY BOOKS

Library of Congress Cataloging-in-Publication Data

Goodman, Dr. Gary S.
   101 things parents should know before volunteering to coach their kids' sports
teams / Dr. Gary S. Goodman.
      p.   cm.
   Includes index.
   ISBN 0-8092-9871-6
   1. Sports for children—Coaching.   2. Parenting.   I. Title: One hundred one
things parents should know before volunteering to coach their kids' sports teams.
   II. Title: One hundred and one things parents should know before volunteering to
coach their kids' sports teams.   III. Title.
GV709.24.G66   2000
796'.07'7—dc21   99-53839
                                                                                   CIP

Cover photographs copyright © Eyewire, Inc.
Cover and interior design by Rattray Design

Published by Contemporary Books
A division of NTC/Contemporary Publishing Group, Inc.
4255 West Touhy Avenue, Lincolnwood (Chicago), Illinois 60712-1975 U.S.A.
Copyright © 2000 by Dr. Gary S. Goodman
Printed in the United States of America
International Standard Book Number: 0-8092-9871-6

00 01 02 03 04 05 MV 17 16 15 14 13 12 11 10 9 8 7 6 5 4 3 2 1

To my wife, best friend, and colleague, Dr. Deanne Goodman, and to our wonderful daughter and athlete, Amanda Leigh Goodman. Without them, I would never have known the pleasures of parenting or of coaching.

I am also very grateful to all of those volunteer coaches and parents who made my childhood sparkle.

Contents

Acknowledgments

I would like to express my appreciation to the entire publishing team at NTC/Contemporary Publishing Group. Special thanks go to editors Kara Leverte and Danielle Egan-Miller, and my project editor, Heidi Bresnahan.

Introduction

APPROXIMATELY FORTY MILLION American girls and boys will play extracurricular sports this year. Organized and conducted largely by parent-volunteers, these activities can build character, strengthen relationships, and add immeasurably to the fabric of everyday life.

Unfortunately, they can also create situations that elicit some of the worst personality flaws and most outrageous behaviors from parents, coaches, and kids. Instead of serving, these activities can scar.

While there are many excellent sports programs and leagues, until now there haven't been any general-purpose books to prepare volunteer-parents to handle the ins and outs and highs and lows of coaching and staffing these activities. With the proper guidance, we can all have fun, help our children to develop, and make a substantial contribution to our communities.

This book contains 101 pointers. Ideally, you should review them *before* you sign on to coach a team. After reading this primer, you could decide that coaching isn't a good fit for you.

If you have already taken the plunge and become a coach, however, this book will still deliver a lot of solid insights and valuable tips. These are just a few of the questions we'll raise and address:

- How important is winning? You'll learn about the YMCA's excellent Y-Winners basketball program in which there is no score keeping.

- Should our chief concern be the teaching of physical skills, mental abilities, or values such as teamwork and sportsmanship?

- Should the best players be allowed more playing time than others?

- How should coaches be screened and selected?

- What codes of conduct should leagues adopt for parental, player, and coaching demeanor?

- How can we get everyone to cooperate and to joyfully share responsibilities?

- What are some proven tips for motivating your players in practices and games?

- What's the best way to break in to coaching?

- When should you scale back your involvement or bow out of coaching?

Approximately one in five parents of players will participate in coaching or serve as a team parent. I hope this book will reach a number of them and start a healthy dialogue that can help all of us and our children to have a positive and warmly treasured sports experience.

The book is divided into twelve parts. Poke around here and there and read what's most important to you first. You can always go back and read the pointers in sequence when you have the time.

One more thing before I turn you loose: While I have coached three different sports and have been involved for years, I'm not perfect, as you'll discover by turning these pages. I've made plenty of mistakes. I hope this book will help you to avoid a good number of them so you won't have to constantly learn the hard way and say: "I wish somebody had told me that!"

At the end of the book, you'll find information on how to contact me to tell me whether I was an effective coaches' coach. I hope to hear from you.

Until then, happy reading . . . and *Go, team*!

—*GSG*
Glendale, California

101 THINGS Parents SHOULD KNOW BEFORE VOLUNTEERING TO Coach THEIR KIDS' Sports Teams

PART I

Breaking into Coaching

I.

Can You Predict What Sort of Coach You'll Become?

You MIGHT SAY I'm a "thinking coach." I love to strategize and to figure out which players will do the best at particular positions. I also like to anticipate what the opposing coaches are going to do. Like a chess player, I'm happiest when I can think ahead two or three moves.

Although I am athletic, and I like to practice with my team, I see coaching as primarily an intellectual exercise. Had a fortune-teller told me that the mental game would be the most significant aspect of my style, I wouldn't have believed it. I expected to be a coach who was going to emphasize drills and mechanics.

Don't get me wrong—I do stress those as well. It's just that my gift, if I may be so bold as to claim one, turned out to be in the area of plotting and planning. I get a real thrill out of the mental maneuvers.

Like the soldier who has never tasted battle—yet who is about to— you never quite know how you'll react to the challenges of coaching before you're thrust into the situation. You may think that you're mild- mannered and soft-spoken, until you hear the whistle and your team takes the court against an opponent for the first time. Suddenly, you become the loudest extrovert in town. Your friends gawk at your behavior with utter astonishment.

I'm not saying there's anything wrong with that. Your unexpected ver- balizations could be appropriate to the situation and fit the needs of your team. But you'll never quite know you have it in you until it starts roar- ing or, perhaps, meowing out.

For instance, I know a number of people who are tigers in business but who are kittens when it comes to correcting their players. Instead of saying anything that could be misconstrued or nick someone's ego, they prefer to remain silent. This trait might make them well liked, but it could get in the way of developing the abilities of players.

I also know other coaches who are just the opposite. Off the field, they're shy and reserved, but when games are in progress or when speaking to their troops, they're bold and effective leaders.

This you-won't-know-it-until-you-do-it phenomenon is much like parenting. When my wife was expecting, I remember saying to my female colleagues and clients that becoming a papa "isn't going to change me very much."

To a person, they laughed and replied, "Sure, Gary!" They knew what I didn't—that parenting can change *everything*, and often for the better.

So, enjoy what you see emerging from the hidden depths of your character. This other personality could be one of the biggest rewards you'll get from coaching.

2.

Try Assisting First

THERE ARE SOME first-rate pleasures in being a second banana—at least in coaching.

For one thing, if you're an assistant coach, you'll have fewer duties and responsibilities. It's analogous to being an employee instead of the owner. When "quitting time" comes, nobody expects you to hang around if you're just another soul on the payroll. But if you're the boss, your work is never, ever completely done.

For another thing, head coaches receive almost all of the complaint letters from angry parents. In addition, they have to attend league meetings, issue uniforms, and monitor myriad details. And they're always on call, for one crisis or another.

Head coaches also take the heat when the team loses, and when parents feel that their offspring have been relegated to the "worst" playing positions. By comparison, assistants live relatively placid lives. They can occasionally skip practices to attend to important business or family matters. They can even take a frivolous midseason vacation or a precious game-day off to play golf—whatever that is. (I know this is all true, because my second and third in command have done all of these things—with nary an apology.)

While the head coach has to become the disciplinarian and to sternly enforce time restrictions during water breaks and other functions, an assistant can play the role of the "good cop," who provides a sympathetic ear to aggrieved players.

In fact, being an assistant is a lot like being a favorite aunt or uncle. You can show up for the happy occasions, like birthdays and graduations and family get-togethers, but you get a free pass on having to deal with the tougher rites of passage, which are the bread and butter of parenting.

One of my favorite comedic lines comes from Mel Brooks's movie *History of the World, Part One*. After doing something completely capricious, Brooks's regal character smugly faces the camera and declares: "It's good to be king!"

Well, when it comes to coaching, it's often better to be assistant king—at least for a while. By being second banana, you can observe as the head person makes error after error, for which you don't have to pay. If you're smart, you'll learn from these miscues, and your wisdom will serve you well if and when you become number one.

It's possible that you will like assisting so much that you never elect to step up to the top spot. Ultimately, you may retire from this form of community service as a slightly happier person for the experience.

There's nothing wrong with turning down an offer to become a head coach. If you're unsure whether you're ready to assume the *big* responsibility, I suggest you wait for another season before making the leap.

3.

What Were *Your* Early Sports Experiences Like?

Were you a successful athlete as a kid? Are you the one who made the memorable catch or hit the incredible home run when the game was on the line?

Were you so talented that you *almost* made it to the majors?

Or, were your abilities just run-of-the-mill?

I think your early sports experiences will definitely inform your coaching style, in the same sense that our parenting styles are affected by our childhood experiences.

If you were a great player, you'll likely:

- understand and pay more attention to your star players. You might help them to develop even more skills, because you'll be able to relate to them.

- place higher demands on the entire team.

- be impatient when your best players don't "deliver," and prematurely write off the potential of your average kids and underperformers.

- be tempted to micromanage games by inserting lots of signs and putting on numerous plays. You'll only reluctantly let the kids simply take the field and play.

- be hard on yourself, and possibly on your players, after your team has flamed out in defeat.

If, while reading this description, you thought of a "type A" personality—one that is driven and who drives others—you're on the right track. If you were an excellent athlete, it almost goes without saying that you're a take-charge and take-no-prisoners type of competitor.

But what if you weren't a top-flight performer on the field? What kind of coach might you become?

If you're coaching kids, you may be more effective than the type A types. Here are the reasons:

- You'll be attuned to your average and below-average achievers. Chances are that you'll invest the majority of your attention in bringing them up to speed, while figuring that the highfliers can take care of themselves.

- You will tend to be less demanding because the team won't be seen as a reflection of your personal sports capabilities.

- You'll be more patient when your team underperforms.

- When the kids take the field, you'll really let *them* take it, and keep it.

- You'll let defeats come and go without making them significant events in your life or in the lives of your players.

You may not extract every last ounce of effort from everyone all the time, but you'll be more fun to be around. Will this make you a better coach?

For kids, yes. For the majors—maybe not.

But that was never your ambition, right?

4.

Welcome to Your Second Full-Time Job!

COACHING IS INCREDIBLY time consuming, even if you're very, very careful in managing your time. You can blow more hours than a ten-year-old can popping quarters into machines at the local arcade. In fact, you might consider it a second full-time job.

How can this be? Let's do a little math. Time commitments will vary from sport to sport, but here's the typical week I had when I managed Little League for the first year.

MONDAY: THREE HOURS

I'd invest a couple of hours reviewing our prior week's practices and games. I'd also make up various batting orders and fielding assignments in preparation for the current week's games. I'd then call the parents to remind them of the game and practice schedules for the week.

TUESDAY: FOUR HOURS

Tuesday was often one of our two game days. So, I'd invest another hour in mental preparation while sketching out our strategy. I'd arrive at the field an hour before the game. If a kid needed a ride, I'd tack on an extra half hour to arrange the pickup.

Games lasted an hour and a half, but with the postgame snack and discussion, you could figure on investing two. Then, if you had to drop off a kid or baby-sit until a parent arrived, this could add another half hour.

WEDNESDAY: TWO HOURS

I'd think through the events of the prior day's game: Who stepped up and delivered a great performance, and why? How come my sluggers' bats were conspicuously silent? Is there any reason we can't lay down a bunt midway through the season? Should I redesign our practices to emphasize this fundamental aspect of the game? Who should I have on the pitcher's mound on Saturday?

You might wonder how anyone can consume two hours in thought about these matters, but you'll be amazed at how easy it is for time to blissfully pass when you're enmeshed in strategy.

Anyway, you don't sit down for the exclusive purpose of investing two hours this way. The game makes you its captive. You'll invest the two hours on any given Wednesday because your competitiveness and desire to do a good job unconsciously force you to.

THURSDAY: THREE HOURS

It's a practice day, so you'll invest an hour preparing your practice strategy and two hours at the practice. (The practice lasts for one and a half hours, but you need to allow fifteen minutes to arrive early and another fifteen to depart later.)

FRIDAY: TWO HOURS

You're planning Saturday's big game while daydreaming about being appointed manager of this year's all-star team. Time certainly flies!

SATURDAY: FOUR HOURS

It's another game day. (See Tuesday for details.)

SUNDAY: TWO HOURS

(You never really get a day off.) A parent calls you to say her daughter's uniform doesn't fit correctly. You suggest she have it tailored. A fellow coach calls you to tell you he'll be golfing in the desert for the week, or skiing because the powder is absolutely irresistible. You're also trying to remember what move you made during yesterday's game that gave you that lower-back strain.

Oh, I nearly forgot! Add transportation time to the calculation, as well as time to change from your work clothes into sports outfits. This will easily affix another three hours to your weekly commitment. Plus, you'll have league meetings along with emergency visits to the sporting goods store to replace equipment, adding another hour or two.

So, how many hours do we have here? By my count, we're up to twenty-five.

But I've left out another factor: You're going to discuss your sport, your players, your coaching style, and a number of related subjects with your family and anyone else who will lend you an ear. Add an hour a day for that, at minimim, and we're up to thirty-two.

Of course, how could I leave out the sleep you'll lose while worrying about who is spreading that nasty rumor that you're really a frustrated, failed pro player who is taking out his or her shortcomings on the players? Add slightly more than an hour a night for this and for being too excited to get to sleep, and we're up to *forty hours*.

Yep, it's your second full-time job.

5.

Is There Such a Thing as a Great Coach?

YOU'VE PROBABLY HAD a lot of coaches in your lifetime. There were physical education teachers, coaches in organized sports, as well as your parents, older siblings, and even the friends you hung out with. Each of them had pointers for you.

But did you have any *great* coaches? These would be the ones you raved about. Simply being in their presence aroused your winner's chemistry. These people made you feel that you were an all-star. Every one of your at bats, goal kicks, or baskets was going to be the one that would win it all.

Even if you blew a play, your coach helped you to feel that you were constantly improving. It was as if your skills were being tugged upward on a *Star Trek* tractor beam. When you screwed up, he or she would help you to shrug it off, get your head back into the contest, and then go on to do your best.

I had a great coach. Irv helped me to get much better in a very short time. At the grand age of twelve, he was only two years my senior, but he was the one who got me ready for Little League.

Irv was one of our town's shorter athletes. Making up in enthusiasm and hustle what he lacked in size, he started all four years on our high school basketball team. He was quick and wily and could fake opponents out of their shoes.

I'd play him one-on-one at the playground, and he'd just run circles around me. In addition to the skills I've already mentioned, Irv was remarkably tough-minded for a kid. But these were merely his playing strengths.

What made him an effective coach? How did he help me to become permanently better at baseball? How was I able to enjoy a quantum leap in skills? For the answer, we flash forward to the day I tried out for Little League.

Each kid was required to catch a fly ball. The grown-up who hit mine belted it so hard that he thought it was impossible to catch. As soon as his bat struck the ball, he shouted, "Forget it!"

But, because of Irv's conditioning, I was already turned around and running full speed after it. Every kid prays to have a great tryout, and here was my chance. I kept running, looked over my shoulder, shot out my glove, and pulled in the ball.

Without hesitating, I tucked my glove into my body and somersaulted toward the left-field fence. When I leaped back to my feet and showed everyone that I still had the ball, an audible "Wow!" erupted from the sidelines. And then, spontaneous applause and cheering broke out.

That day, I was drafted by the Dodgers, and my best friend, Bobby, made the Cardinals. He was an aspiring pitcher, and I boasted to him, "The first time I face you, I'm going to hit a home run over the center-field fence, just like Babe Ruth!" He just shook his head.

A year later, as a game was about to draw to a close, Bobby was brought in as a relief pitcher to face me. I smiled knowingly, while pointing to center field. He surpressed a grin.

On a two-and-one count, I reached for an outside pitch and launched a rocket into dead center field. It hung in the air, seemingly forever, and then dropped outside the fence for a home run. Again, Bobby shook his head, but this time it was in astonishment.

I knew I could do it. Irv had taught me the two most important ingredients in becoming a sports champ. One was unrelenting hard work. The second was visualization. He said I had to see myself making the big plays. I had to believe in myself, and tell myself, over and over, that I had what it took.

He went on to play in the Chicago White Sox organization. I'm not sure if he ever left a mark on the majors, but he had a huge impact on me.

So, is there such a thing as a great coach? Absolutely. They come in all shapes and sizes and ages. But they do seem to stress two essential things:

1. Work harder than anybody else.

2. Expect great things from yourself.

6.

How Much Sports Savvy Should a Coach Have?

When I was recruited to be an assistant coach in soccer, I knew frightfully little about the sport. Sure, I had played it as a kid—as one of many sports that we cycled through in physical education classes—but as an adult, I couldn't distinguish a midfielder from a forward.

Frankly, my ignorance scared me. I had forgotten most of the rules of the game, except the fact that the goalie is the only player allowed to use his or her hands to touch the ball. I was much more conversant with the ins and outs of baseball, football, and basketball, by comparison. I thought I'd be a complete screwup when I had to give pointers to the players.

And, to be honest with you, it took me about three or four games before I got the hang of the rules and a solid feeling for basic soccer strategy. But by midseason, I was making major contributions to the team.

I found that being an observant novice had its advantages. The head coach, who was a delight to work with, allowed me to do a lot, but he also respected my lack of experience and self-confidence. By watching, I was able to see patterns that he missed despite his expertise.

For instance, we had two players who were very gifted. He appointed one a center forward, and the other a center midfielder. This turned out to be an underutilization of their speed and scoring abilities. I suggested we have them both play forwards, while developing the setup strengths of our other players. It worked, and we snapped a losing streak.

Buoyed by that win, I urged him to put our speediest player at center defense. She was awesome at preventing our opponents from scoring, and we won again. In fact, we became the Knockout Tournament Champions, despite the fact that we had suffered through an early-season slump.

The head coach was great. He was open to my suggestions, and when they started having an impact, he encouraged me to come up with even more. I was happy to comply.

In our end-of-the-year party, he acknowledged my "gift for strategy." Imagine that. I didn't know up from down at the start of the season, but by its finale, I was a "genius."

Well, not really, but I felt a heck of a lot more capable. And so will you, no matter how ignorant you may be of the refinements of the sport you choose to coach—or that chooses you. By simply paying attention and applying your horse sense, you'll make a bigger contribution than you ever imagined.

And you'll have a lot of fun doing it!

7.

How to Handle the Physical Challenges of Coaching

WHEN I BECAME a brand-new parent, I came across a simple tip about how to play with one's infant. It was expressed this way: "If you're not down on the floor with them, you're not really playing."

I hadn't spent much time on the floor as an adult, so this didn't seem like such a great idea. But soon, I confirmed the wisdom contained in this adage. It felt a lot more like playing when I descended from my perch on the couch to the carpet. And my child seemed to think so as well.

A similar principle applies to coaching. You're not really coaching unless you're in there with your players, passing balls around, shooting a few hoops, and demonstrating exactly how they should execute their fast breaks. Words alone are poor substitutes for actions.

Now that I've said this, you should be aware of just how much of a toll this kind of physical exertion is going to exact: **Coaching is going to exhaust you, at least at the beginning of a season.** You'll activate long-dormant muscles, which will cry out for relief. That's the good news.

The bad news is that you'll be tempted to cut back on your physical commitment. Your body will ask you for more and more rest during practices and games, but don't cave in to its wishes. Instead, force yourself to get into better shape.

I suggest you join a gym, take up jogging, or even do some form of martial arts to condition your body. In other words, do an additional form of exercise so the sport you coach won't keep exhausting you.

This seems like a lot of trouble to go to, doesn't it? Believe me, you'll be happy you rose to the challenge. You'll get into better all-around shape, and you'll have more self-confidence. And because you're teaching by example, your players will also hold you in higher regard.

I'd start this process well before the season begins. That way, it won't be an imposition for you to accommodate the extra physical challenges that are ushered in by coaching a sport. Getting off the couch is more fun anyway!

8.

Wanted: More Women Coaches!

You may have noticed: women's sports are booming. But so far, we aren't seeing enough women in coaching. This is especially the case in kids' sports. I have coached my daughter and her friends in soccer, basketball, and baseball. When I look at the roster of fellow coaches, that's by and large what I see—only fellows.

Why more women aren't coaching their daughters is anybody's guess. One definite possibility is that many of them bear the primary responsibility for performing other parental duties, so they don't have any time left to dedicate to coaching.

Perhaps men find it easier to get release time from their employers to perform coaching duties. Or, it could be that some women believe that males know more about sports, and thus they defer to them. Maybe some feel they would be unwelcome, so they stay away.

I want to send a clear message to moms: **You're wanted and needed in coaching.** You'll bring definite pluses with you, including:

- You'll be a positive role model with whom girls, especially, can identify.

- If you coach your son's team, you'll help to overcome limiting stereotypes of women. It's important for boys to see women in positions of leadership throughout society, not simply at home and in the working world.

- You may be more inclined to perceive, respect, and accommodate the feelings of players and parents. For example, after witnessing an injury, too many male coaches are inclined to reflexively bark out "Shake it off—you'll be all right," without taking the time to inquire into the severity of the pain that the child is experiencing.

I've noticed that moms who coach tend to be much more sensitive to the potential complications involved in injuries and accidents.

- Sports will be a fun outlet and a channel for your competitive tendencies, which may be supressed in other areas of life.

- You'll have a lot more to talk about at the dinner table with your kids!

My daughter was lucky to have not one, but two, female coaches during her first soccer season. I thought they were very good motivators, and I was glad they were the ones to welcome my small-fry to the sport.

We need a lot more like them. So, if you're a mom, please take the plunge. We'll all be glad you did!

9.

Are You Coaching the Right Age-Group?

When Bill was in his late teens, he nearly made it to the major leagues. Now that he has a child, he can't wait to get involved in coaching.

Because he knows so much about the game, he has the potential to become a great coach. But he absolutely must make sure to coach the right age-group. If he doesn't, he's going to be frustrated, and he's also going to make a lot of other people miserable along the way.

It's a fact that the best coaches for young kids are the most patient. Surprisingly, for older kids, it may be the other way around.

What am I saying? Isn't patience a virtue for every coach to possess? Not necessarily.

Little kids can't be pushed to perform without hurting their feelings. They need an extremely supportive environment that makes nearly everything they do in sports seem like a huge accomplishment. We can't offer them too much positive reinforcement for trying. I'm speaking here of kids who are eight years old and younger—kids who are playing T-ball.

But when the players have to hit pitched balls, when games are being scored, and there are acknowledged differences between winning and losing, the ante is increased, quickly and substantially. By nine, ten, and especially eleven and twelve, kids know most of the important rules involved in their chosen sports. They also run greater risks of being injured while participating. The stakes are higher, and sporting events take on more of the flavor of serious competitions.

At this stage, coaches need to show some *impatience*, particularly with kids who are goofing off or who aren't playing up to their potential. From a skills-development perspective, players need to receive a *balance* of positive and corrective feedback so that they'll grow, both on the field and off.

Because the pace of contests is faster, there is no time to coddle them. They need to be directed quickly and firmly, particularly if they're standing in the batter's box, facing a pitcher who is hurling an object at eighty miles per hour or faster. A coach needs to be able to bark out: "Move back in the box!" and to have the kids and parents accept this direction without taking offense.

If you're not good at showing impatience and being a bit of the drill sergeant, you should reconsider your decision to coach kids who are nine and above. By the same token, if your supreme virtue is patience, then please get involved with the younger set.

They need you, they'll appreciate you, and above all, you'll appreciate them. If, on the other hand, you constantly are being admonished by parents and officials to "lighten up," you may be well advised to wait until your kid is a little older before volunteering to coach your next team.

10.

Yes, You *Are* a Baby-Sitting Service!

I WOULD GUESS that at least half of the parents you'll meet as a coach will have their kids playing sports, at least in part, because these diversions keep the little ones busy. It really doesn't matter to these moms or dads whether their offspring are playing soccer, or softball, or rugby. They just want them out of their hair for a few hours at a time. So, in effect, you're providing them with a cheap baby-sitting service. It's a pity, but I think you'll find that it's true. Don't get me wrong—no one will say this in so many words, but they will reveal it through their conduct.

For instance, there are parents who never stay during practices. They'll just drop off their kids and ask you, "When is practice over?" Then, they may return late, leaving you to hang around the court or field long after the official conclusion of the get-together.

Other parents will not only never stay for practices but also won't come to games, either. In other words, their level of commitment is next to zilch. Again, up to 50 percent of a team's parents will be like this. So, what can you do about it?

Not much. I accept it for what it is. And like the best baby-sitters, I still try to create an environment that is fun, stimulating, and one in which my little wards learn.

After all, it's not their fault that their parents are somewhere else. And baby-sitting is an important and honorable activity, don't you agree?

II.

Make Sure *You're* Having Enough Fun

Do you know what happens to folks who do everything they can for other people but who ignore their own needs?

They tend to break down sooner or later.

This definitely applies to coaches, who occasionally have to be everything to their teams. Amid strategizing, finding time for practices and games, dragging equipment around, making sure someone is accurately scoring the games, managing the team parent so that snacks arrive on a reliable basis, and chauffeuring kids to and from games, we can easily feel overwhelmed and underappreciated.

There's only one way to prevent a feeling of burnout from sneaking up on you: **Build enough fun into the process for yourself!**

I do this by giving myself a chance to actually play some of the sport that I'm coaching. In soccer practice, I may play goalie, while another coach does likewise for our scrimmage mates. While I hold back some of my playing intensity, I still try to get in a good workout. If I'm not sweating along with my players at some point in our practices, I'm simply not having enough fun.

In baseball, I may pitch or catch during batting practice. Or, I'll fill in somewhere in the outfield. I'll go where I can do the most good.

Sometimes, I'll jog a few laps with the team before the game. I also make a point of warming up my pitchers, and I like to spend a little time playing catch with the youngest players so that I can get them involved, while offering a pointer here and there.

I think it's helpful for the kids to see a coach practicing what we're preaching. They can model after us, and it's always more effective to show them a good bunt than to just give them a description of one.

I also try to get my fellow coaches involved in playing. I can see how it loosens them up, and the players appreciate the effort, even if we occasionally embarrass ourselves!

To give myself another excuse to play, I'll invite the parents, sisters, and brothers of our players to bring their gloves and bats and join us in a scrimmage. Invariably, this is fun for everybody, and it makes the team more cohesive.

Occasional "family days" will encourage parents who haven't been coming to many games or practices to show up more often. Fun begets more fun.

Just make sure you're building enough of it into games and practices for yourself.

12.

Should You Coach Two
Teams at a Time?

LET'S SAY YOU have two children. One of them is seven, so she's in a T-ball league. The other is nine and ready to step up to Little League. They both want you to coach their teams. What should you do?

If you say yes to one and no to the other, it may seem that you're showing favoritism toward the lucky child who has Mom or Dad for a coach. Yet, if you consent to directing two teams, you're going to be taking on a huge time and energy commitment.

Let's examine the options. First, let me say that I think it's unbelievably stressful to be the head coach for two teams during the same season. When you're the top dog, you have to pay attention to too many details. You're in charge of strategy, and you're expected to attend each practice and game.

In terms of time commitment, as established earlier in #4, coaching one team is often a full-time job. Unfortunately, there are no "scale economies" to be realized in coaching two. So, coaching a pair of teams could be the equivalent of taking on two additional full-time jobs.

If you already work at a job where you're committed for 40 hours, you could be looking at a total outlay, between work and athletics, of 120 hours per week. There are only 168 hours in anybody's week. This will leave you 6.85 hours to sleep each night, and you may not even have time to brush your teeth.

Perhaps I'm exaggerating. Nonetheless, something will have to give, whether it's your regular job, other elements of your personal life, or the actual time you dedicate to coaching. You're burning the candle at three ends!

You have another option if you feel you must be involved with both teams: you can be an assistant coach for both, which would exclude a lot of the administrative and strategic burdens. Just by doing this, you recover about 25 hours per week—and less heat will be placed on you to lead your teams to victory.

If you occasionally have to miss a game or a practice, you'll probably have the head coach and another assistant on whom to rely to pick up the slack. And your absences, while unfortunate, won't be nearly as conspicuous as they would be if you were the big chief.

There is a thin line between feeling fulfilled as a volunteer and feeling overwhelmed and resentful that you've taken on too many challenges. If you allow your ego to propel you into too many commitments, you'll burn out, and you could be remembered as merely a "one-season wonder."

Another option is to become a parent-helper to both teams. Cut a deal with the coaches that you'll be there to assist in any way you can when you can make it to practices and games. This way, your actual commitment will be a variable that you'll always control. You'll still be very visible to both of your children, and you won't be letting either one down.

A final option is not to coach at all. Simply coming to as many games and practices as you can will mean a lot to your kids. They need cheerleaders, and you can aspire to become one of the best.

This would leave you with time to do other significant things, like getting a full night's sleep every now and then.

PART II

Organizing and Coordinating

13.

Meet with Parents Before the Season Begins

MAKE SURE TO schedule a meeting with your players' parents as soon as possible after your roster has been formed. If you don't, you'll miss an all-important opportunity to orchestrate an effective first impression.

Please note that I didn't say your goal is to convey a "good" impression. That would be pleasant, but our goal at the first meeting isn't to "win friends and influence people." It is really about accomplishing four primary goals:

- **You need to let parents know that you're a real human being off the field.**

If they only catch glimpses of you during practices or games, they'll come away with a two-dimensional impression that is little better than a crude stereotype. It's easier to dislike a caricature than a real, flesh-and-blood individual.

- **You need to announce your ground rules and describe your coaching style.**

If you're somewhat rough around the edges when it comes to critiquing players, put parents at ease by telling them, "My bark is worse than my bite." On the other hand, if you are slow to anger but can get uncorked once you pass a certain point, tell them, "My bite is actually worse than my bark!" Parents should hear this so they can anticipate your on-the-field reactions.

For instance, most people know that the Indiana University basketball team has a fiery coach in Bobby Knight. This is one guy who doesn't take the game lightly, and he shows a lot of emotion, including rage. If you're about to have your child go to IU for basketball, you need to know what to expect from the coach. Your kid is probably going to be pushed hard, especially if he has a lot of talent or intelligence that he isn't using.

You may not completely agree with Knight's methods, or with coaches who emulate him, but at least you have a right to be on notice when it comes to how he'll conduct his team.

Some coaches do go over the top emotionally. I've done it myself. It happens because we *care* about giving the best performance we can, while eliciting the best from our players. Recently, I was listening to the radio sports guru Jim Rome, who said that the best athletes and managers do get very emotional.

But let's get back to our meeting. When coaching baseball, I might tell parents: "If your child *deliberately* goes against a signal by hitting away when she's been asked to bunt, she'll either be warned on the spot or pulled from the game—if necessary, in the middle of a count."

I *want* parents to challenge me, then and there, if they're not thoroughly comfortable with what I'm saying. This way, we can talk it through, and they can hear even more of my philosophy. By creating clarity, I have a chance of having them support and reinforce the message at home when their kid asks, "Why did Coach Gary take me out of the game?" They can simply reply, "You swung at the ball when you were given a clear 'bunt' sign—that's why. He has corrected you on that a number of times." End of discussion.

If you don't offer a formal parent briefing, which covers their expectations and yours, each decision you make will be subject to being challenged by disappointed kids and surprised parents. Believe me, life is far too short for the backward-looking, self-justifying behavior in which you'll get mired if you don't have the earliest possible powwow with your moms and dads.

• **A meeting will also smoke out the parents from whom you can expect hassles.**

My suggestion to you is to recruit these "problem parents" for special duties as soon as you can. For example, if you have identified potential complainers, do the opposite of what your impulses tell you to do. Don't recoil from them; talk to them as much as you can.

In fact, pay more *positive* attention to malcontents than you do to the other parents. Ask them to do you a favor. Have them help out with something during the first practice. Short on players? Have them alternate at goalie until the rest of your players straggle in.

Once you assign them to a positive and supportive role, they won't have the time or the desire to torpedo your efforts because that would overtly diminish their own effectiveness.

• **The organizational meeting is where you take care of the formal assignments, as well.**

At least one person needs to serve as a team parent, to handle coordinations and communications during the season. (The team parent's duties are explained in #24.) I suggest you recruit two people. This way, you can have one serve this year, while the second assists and prepares to take over official duties next year.

Just as a good business has a succession plan that provides for who will step up to serve in the absence of a key person, we should have plans for the ongoing administration of our sports teams. This is why I urge you to groom multiple people for essential roles.

By the time of your meeting, if you haven't already chosen assistant coaches, you'll need to recruit some. Don't leave that room without securing two, and preferably three, commitments. You have to make it quite clear, if volunteers aren't readily coming forward, that a sports team cannot function effectively with only one coach.

In most leagues involving youngsters, parents rotate in the responsibility of bringing snacks and refreshments to games for the players. Pass around a sign-up list, and make sure everyone assumes his or her share of the responsibilities.

Perhaps 50 percent of your parents won't want to help in any way. By having your meeting, in which you get *everybody* involved from the get-go, you'll put a lot of social pressure on these people, and you'll get a lot more from them than you would through nonstop requests after the season has begun.

14.

Tardiness, Absences, and Attendance Policies

I AM A reformed latecomer.

I used to think nothing of being late to parties, to appointments, to classes as a student. But then, everything changed. I was selected to become a member of an elite navy training group, and one of its core requirements was stated this way: "Hit your time targets!"

Arrive at the site on time. Start the program on time, and then stop on time. No excuses were allowed. We were the masters of the clock, and we were expected to understand that you can't get anything important done with a group unless everyone respects punctuality.

A famous comedian said that 90 percent of success in life is attributable to showing up on time. I think he was joking, but he's not far off the mark. If you were a teacher or a business manager, who do you think would make a better impression—the person who was always "fashionably late" or the eager one—who made a point to be present and ready a few minutes early?

I've said it in various places in this book, and I can't emphasize it enough: When we're coaching, we're teaching values. Let one of them be the value of showing up on time.

That said, what should we do about chronic latecomers or absent kids? First of all, they're late, as a general rule, because their parents are late. Mom or Dad thinks it's OK to treat time in a sloppy way or is overbooked with responsibilities. Either way, the parents should make some adjustments in their calendars.

Make a clear point of saying at the outset that you're a "stickler" about punctuality. If parents know before the start of the season that they're going to be chronically late or absent, then they should reconsider having their child play on the team.

There are three crucial reasons supporting this position:

1. If kids are late or absent, they'll miss the instructions necessary to play their positions, and you don't have the time to conduct separate tutorials for them.

2. Arriving late is disruptive and distracting to other kids. It takes their attention and focus away when one of their peers is time insensitive.

3. Tardiness and absences are insulting to the coaches, to the team, and to other parents.

Edward T. Hall, in his books on nonverbal communication, *The Hidden Dimension* and *The Silent Language*, says, "Time talks, and space speaks." How we handle time sends a significant message to others. In my view, the latecomer or chronically absent child says "This activity isn't important enough to me to be on time."

In order that you will appear to be fair and objective, I suggest you generate some explicit rules. You could decide that a kid who is late to three practices or games will be prevented from being in the starting lineup of a game. A kid who is late to five practices and/or games will be suspended from playing in an entire game.

Unexcused absences can be handled as you feel appropriate. But let's agree on this: You'll tend to elicit more of what you reward, and less of what you punish. If you set no policy and you're silent with regard to chronic absences and tardiness, you'll implicitly reward these counterproductive behaviors.

Naturally, exceptions should be made for legitimate illnesses. But I'd be reluctant to look the other way if a family decides to take numerous weekend vacations that prevent a child from attending team events. If they want to take off, let them disrupt someone else's team—or league, for that matter.

15.

How to Get Other Parents to Joyously Participate

AT ONE TIME, futurists predicted that we were becoming a leisure society. They prophesied that we'd have so much time on our hands that we wouldn't know what to do with it.

Today, those predictions seem ludicrous because most of us feel pressed to accomplish more than ever in less time. So, on one level, it would seem unrealistic to tell you that you can get parents more involved with helping their kids' sports teams. But you can, and you'll be doing them a favor if you succeed in recruiting them.

Why should you bother getting others to help you out? Here are a few reasons:

- If they're occupied with something constructive, they'll have less time to be destructive. This especially applies to those who think they know more about coaching or sports than you do.

- When seasons begin, time shrinks. You just won't have the time to make phone calls, plan end-of-season parties, shop for replacement equipment, and do any number of little things that you thought you'd have plenty of opportunity to do.

- You'll be cultivating the same involved parents for future seasons, when they may step up to becoming assistant or head coaches.

- You'll have a support group when other parents become upset with your coaching style or decisions.

Why should parents allow themselves to be recruited? Here are a few incentives:

- It's fun to contribute.

- It gives them a welcome break from working.

- They get closer to their children.

- They develop skills they didn't know they had.

- Just as it's said that kids are only young once, parents are in a position to help in this special way during only a limited window of time.

- They feel they're needed, which helps to elevate their self-esteem.

As I wrote these two lists, I noticed that it was easier to create the second one—the reasons parents might want to help out. The lesson: They may get more out of helping than you'll get from their help!

This shouldn't come as a surprise, I suppose, if you endorse the old saying: "It's impossible to help somebody else without helping yourself." So, don't be bashful about asking for parental help. You'll be doing *everyone* a big favor!

16.

A Sample Preseason Letter to Parents

IF YOU END up being the manager or head coach of a team, I urge you to send a preseason letter to all parents as soon as the roster is made available to you by your league. This letter, which can follow the contours of the sample provided here, will accomplish several purposes:

- It will announce the first parents' meeting. (See #13 for tips on how this meeting should be conducted.) We really need to meet parents as a group so that everyone can communicate eye-to-eye. A letter, on the other hand, is more formal and seems somewhat official. That's good because we need to get their attention right away.

- It will demonstrate your credibility. You'll seem organized and ready to roll. A friendly but take-charge demeanor is what you want to convey at this point.

- It will be a formal request for helpers. Parents will come to the meeting knowing that they'll be tapped to participate. And some will even call you beforehand to volunteer.

- It will be your first chance to communicate the importance of observing certain rules, such as those pertaining to attendance. They'll hear more about this at the meeting, but you need to use the letter as a method of planting the seed.

- It will formally open the communication channels between you and your players' parents.

So, here's my shot at the preseason letter. Add to it if you like, or compose your own. But whatever you do, please do yourself a favor by distributing one in a timely manner.

Work phone: 555-1234
Home phone: 555-4321
Cellular phone: 555-7890
Fax: 555-4761
E-mail: coachgary@wildcats.com

[Date]

To: All Parents of The Wildcats

From: Coach Gary [Gary Goodman]

Subject: Welcome to the [year] Season!

Ah, the grass is getting greener, the birds are singing, and it's time once more to play Little League Baseball! Let me be the first to welcome you to our new season.

I'm looking forward to seeing you at our organizational meeting on [date and time] at [location]. This year, we'll need the following helpers:

1. Two TEAM PARENTS, who will organize the snack schedule and the end-of-the-season party, as well as other details

2. An ASSISTANT COACH (No experience required!)

3. Two BACKUP COACHES, who will occasionally help out at practices and who will be able to assist the manager when other coaches are absent or tied up.

There are involvement opportunities available to everyone, so please let me know if you'd like to help in some capacity.

A prominent comedian once said that "Ninety percent of success in life is showing up on time." Let me echo that idea. It's imperative that we all try our best to be punctual and to attend as many practices and games as we can. If your work or other activities prevent you from keeping up with the team's schedule, please let me know, and we'll establish some car pools.

If you know of a conflict that will prevent your player from attending a substantial number of team events, or that will make him or her chronically late, let's discuss it right away!

At the top of this page, you'll see my work, home, and cellular phone numbers, as well as my fax number and E-mail address. If anything comes up that you'd like to discuss, I'll do my best to be available to you.

At our meeting on [day], I'll have some other important information for you, including the dates and times of our preseason practices. I'm also going to discuss my coaching philosophy and our team's approach to developing the skills of our children. At that time, I'll also distribute some important rules and regulations that parents and other fans will want to observe.

As you know, our overarching purpose is to have fun, but also to teach certain values and skills related to teamwork that will be an advantage to our children for the rest of their lives. We're partners in this, and I look forward to your input, your feedback, and your support.

Working together, I'm sure we'll all have a lot of *fun*!

17.

Distribute a Team
Policies Letter

ONE DRIZZLY AFTERNOON, I arrived at our softball field a little early for our pregame practice. On the field, two highly spirited college teams were battling. Unfortunately, our local college lost, but I was privy to a telling exchange between the coach and one of his players:

"Would you pick up the bats for me, Tracy?" said the coach.

(Silence)

"Would you pick up the *bats* for me, Tracy?" repeated the coach.

(Silence)

"Tracy, please get the *bats* for me, OK?"

"Yeah, OK," Tracy finally replied.

I chatted with the coach after Tracy had meandered over to the bus. I remarked, "Gee, it seems even college-aged kids have to be told things three times before they respond. I thought it was only my twelve-year-olds!"

He grinned and replied, "I *always* have to do that, with everything!"

The coach understood one of the tenets of communication theory quite well: Redundancy works in getting our messages through to other people. We need to repeat ourselves, and this is especially the case when we're coaching or dealing with kids or their parents in a team-related capacity. (Gee, I just repeated myself in this paragraph, didn't I?)

One way to be redundant without being tedious is to exploit a variety of communication channels. I hope that you'll meet with parents at least once before the season begins (see #13 and #16), but this encounter won't be enough contact to convey your points. What else can you do?

Send them a letter that explains the team's policies and procedures.

In your letter, you'll welcome parents and players to the team and to the new season. You'll also credential yourself, indicating how long you've been coaching, if this is one of your strengths. Likewise, if you played college, semipro, or professional sports, say so. If you've been "informally" helping sports teams for years, without having an official coaching title, you could mention that experience.

Then, get into specifics. Discuss the schedule, making sure to point out any irregular times during which certain games or play-offs will be played, such as Sundays. Make it clear that your goal is to have 100 percent attendance at practices and games because this makes being on a team a truly shared experience.

Also make clear that you expect the earliest possible notification if a child can't make it to a practice or game. State how long practices will last and the need for kids to bring water bottles, appropriate equipment, and any other paraphernalia.

If you have any doubt about including a given policy, consult with someone whose opinion you trust. Have your associate read the draft for clarity, tone, and attitude. If the reader sees any red flags, remove or rewrite the offending text.

By using the written channel as well as others, you'll increase the likelihood that your most important policies will be understood, remembered, and upheld.

18.

It's Easy to Line Up Team Sponsors and Financial Support

MOST SPORTS LEAGUES are underfinanced and underequipped. While they may have enough volunteers, they don't have nearly as much support in the form of cash in the till. The good news is that there is absolutely no reason for them to be so destitute.

Lots of local businesses would be more than happy to sponsor teams or to contribute to league coffers if they were asked. There are many, nearly irresistible advantages for those who help their local teams:

• Buying a patch on a uniform that bears the business's name provides ongoing advertising before a local neighborhood population. There aren't many advertising media that local businesses can select that will do the same thing without a lot of "wasted circulation."

Moreover, it is often difficult to place outdoor ads in residential areas because of zoning laws, but when ads are on uniforms or in sports venues, these restrictions ordinarily are relaxed or simply don't apply. So, the sponsor's ad will be seen and processed, and will not be lost amid a lot of competing clutter.

• Generally, people are in a good mood—and are therefore more receptive—when they see a sponsor's name on the caps and uniforms that their children are wearing. After all, they're watching their kids having fun.

• Many people feel a special sense of gratitude for team sponsors. Their support seems benevolent when it is associated with a team. The same "ad" placed in a newspaper could seem overtly commercial and arouse no warm fuzzies in those who see it.

• It's a bargain, in most circumstances, to sponsor a team or to purchase league advertising. In my Little League, for instance, a sponsor is asked for only a few hundred dollars a year. Almost any business can afford that.

An even bigger bargain is a League's yearbook, in which a supporter may run an ad the size of a business card for as little as $45. So, if businesses feel it would be unfair to "favor" one team over another through team sponsorship, they can buy an ad that will benefit the entire league.

So, how can we broaden our base of support? I suggest you drum up support by actually visiting businesses. Ideally, you'll have a fully uniformed player or two in tow to serve as your "visual aids." They'll silently, but vividly, represent the reason you're requesting the business's support.

"Want to know where your money is going, Mr. or Ms. Businessperson? It's going to help them, and a lot of kids like them!"

Face it—kids are cute. The Girl Scouts know this, and I assure you that those who sell cookies while in uniform do much better than those who simply wear their "civvies."

I suspect the primary reason leagues aren't flush with funding is simply ignorance: potential supporters have no clue that helping their local sports teams is a bargain. In addition to doing a good deed, donating in this way gives sponsors smart and targeted advertising as well as positive public relations.

At the same time, parents, coaches, and league officials don't know how *easy* it is to line up support. Literally scores of businesses are ready, willing, and able to help. All we have to do is show them how.

PART III

Selecting Coaches and Team Parents

19.

Handling the Ghosts of Coaches Past

WHEN YOU START to coach any team, including even newly formed ones, you're never completely calling your own shots. You'll have other coaches' and parents' opinions to take into account.

This is to be expected. But you'll also be visited by other, less tangible interlopers: the ghosts of coaches past.

How will you know they're hanging around, if they're ghosts?

You'll know. Kids will say things like, "John, my last coach, said to kick the ball with my toe, and not with the side of my foot!"

If you're not in a patient mood, you'll want to reflexively retort: "Well, John's wrong! I don't know where he got such a stupid idea, but he's 100 percent out-to-lunch on that one. . . . By the way, John's not coaching this team—*I am.*"

That's what you'll *want* to say, because this phantom is leading your little wards astray. He's making them filter your important instructions through the heavy gauze of the past. Undoubtedly, some vital directions will get stuck in the translation.

When I took over as manager of a Little League team, I spent about a half hour introducing my players to our signs for stealing, bunting, and the like. After I had drilled everyone, I gave various kids the chance to play the role of third-base coach—"the Great Giver of Signs."

After each one had fun taking a turn at this baseball version of "cha-rades," one voice whined, "These signs are a lot different from the ones *John* gave us last year. We had a whole notebook of them. I can bring it in, if you like."

"Actually," I said, "I kinda like our new ones." Then, I whispered, "Anyway, a part of having signs is making sure they're kept *secret*, so I'm not sure I want to use signs that have been around too long, where other people may know them, OK?"

To minimize the tendency of kids to incessantly dredge up the past, I suggest having a chat with your group at the first practice. Plan on dedicating about fifteen minutes to discussing what the players feel are some of the best drills that the team used in the past.

Ask the parents if previous coaches incorporated any special rituals that you might benefit from considering. Cover yourself by mentioning that you'll do what you can to employ these tips but that you'll doubtless devise some new ones which may work even better.

Sooner or later, your kids will relax and realize that there's a new sheriff in town—and that's you. "Coach John" will have finally ridden off into the sunset, becoming in the process a fond but more distant memory.

Until that happens, be patient. Realize that someday, you too will be loudly quoted by your former players. It will be your turn to annoy future coaches with *your* wisdom.

Remind yourself of this the next time you want to tell your players how you really feel about having to take pointers from a ghost.

20.

Choose Your Assistants Carefully

IF YOU'RE A new manager or head coach, the first critical job you'll have is selecting an assistant coach or two with whom to work. To save you a tremendous amount of regret, let me describe for you the "Assistant from Hell."

This isn't a person who comes across as mean or malicious. On the contrary, the man or woman is usually a real charmer. By day, you may find such people working in sales or some other "people"-intensive business. In fact, one of their primary motivations for coaching could be to "network" with other parents in order to expand their insurance or real estate client base.

How can you tell off the bat that you'll have trouble with them? Often, they'll reveal their true character with a warning. They'll say: "I'll be happy to help out, but I'm going to miss a game here and there."

This sounds innocent enough, and you really do need a helper, don't you? But right away, you should probe to determine what they mean by "a game here or there." Ask them up front, "Which games or practices do you *know* you're going to miss?"

Get ready to hear a long list—that is, if they're going to fully disclose the immensity of their intended irresponsibility. Some will be forthcoming, and some won't. If only I had asked this question a few seasons ago, I might have heard this answer: "Well, I love to ski and golf. Because half of our games are on Saturdays, I'll miss about five of them, between going to the mountains and the desert."

If I had then probed further—"Do you think you'll miss any practices?"—the response would have been: "Oh, that's right! I nearly forgot— I'll miss about half of them as well. We're swamped at the office, and I just won't be able to break away early enough in the afternoon. You understand, of course . . ."

If you need an assistant coach, you'll desperately want to understand. In fact, you'll rationalize the absences and tell yourself that somehow you'll make do. But believe me, you'll be making a pact with the devil.

One of the keys to running a successful team is being *responsible* to each other. We all have to make sacrifices to bring about positive results. The assistant who believes that he or she can breeze in and out, getting the glory without putting in the long hours, will set an awful example.

Moreover, your pact with this demon will start to bother you. When you're short-handed, and you're watching your supposed assistant slalom down the slopes of your mind, you'll start wishing for avalanches. After practices conclude, with about five hundred yards between you and your car, the bag of bats and balls will weigh heavily on your left arm, cutting into your shoulder. While you're struggling to clutch the helmets with your right hand, you'll imagine your errant helper casually soaking up the rays on the back nine.

But you'll have to blame yourself for not having been clear about the ground rules for being an assistant coach on your team. You didn't say, "I'd love to have you aboard, but I won't be able to justify your absences. I'm sure *you* understand, right?"

If you absolutely must, you can accept help from a parent who is going to be only intermittently present. Just don't make the mistake of giving him or her the formal designation of "Assistant Coach." It will only devalue the title, while stirring resentments. Save it for someone else who may step up to help you. Save it for a parent or other volunteer who is much more reliable and who really deserves this designation, along with the respect and recognition it confers.

21.

Choose Folks Who Won't Compete with Other Coaches

THE OPPOSING COACH yelled toward the umpire, "She's out! She failed to slide at the plate!"

Belatedly, the ump took this observation to heart and declared my player to be out, robbing us of an earned run.

There is a rule in Little League that requires kids to slide into home if the play is going to be close. The goal is a worthy one: to avoid the injuries that can come from total, body-to-body collisions.

A player who fails to slide on a close play *is* out, but these are always judgment calls on the part of umpires. In the same game, an opposing player committed an "automatic-out offense" when she threw her bat all the way to the side of the backstop after punching a single. I resisted the temptation to urge the ump to declare her out because I figured that it was the official's prerogative, and I wasn't going to make a big deal out of it. With certain calls, you figure some will go your way and some will go to your opponents. Plus, it's not fun for a kid to score a run or get a clean base hit, then hear the shocking news that she's out because of a technicality.

Now, two innings later, the opposing coach didn't have the class or the forbearance to look the other way, as I had done.

I blew my top. "Harvey," I boomed, "that's it! I gave you that thrown-bat play, and I didn't tell the umpire how to call it. From here on in, you're getting nothing from me."

It was an interesting moment in softball, to say the least. The stands became silent. Both dugouts were motionless, and the umpire started using the "calm-down-now" double-waving-of-the-hands gesture. I eased off, but my point was made. We were going to be hard to beat from that second forward.

Our team rallied and won by a wide margin. But I paid a big price because relations between old Harv and me were never quite the same.

When our teams played, there was way too much ego on the line. He wanted "payback" for the game we won, and I wanted to show him that our victory that day wasn't a fluke. From the moment of our confrontation, we seemed to make our coaching decisions based more on whether we would defeat each other than improve the skills of the kids.

And I think something was lost amid the acrimony. The games started to become about us—the generals—instead of about the personnel on the field. Like Patton and Rommel, we were more interested in defeating each other's strategy than in the fate of those who counted on us for direction.

Instead of competing with each other, we should have been helping our teams to perform the mechanics of their sport, including the safety-related behaviors of sliding and bat control.

Many of us who coach are former athletes, and we're competitive by nature. That's OK if we compete primarily with ourselves, but we have to appreciate that in coaching kids' sports, competing with fellow coaches isn't a positive practice.

When you select other coaches, be cautious about bringing aboard helpers who seem to be destructively competitive. If they're already aboard, help them to tone it down and stay focused on helping the kids.

22.

How Should Coaches Be Selected?

WE'VE ALL HEARD about or had a negative experience with a coach. It could be a person who had too little patience, or who seemed to hold kids to nearly professional standards. He or she may have screamed too much or empathized too little. What is clear is that the person was a poor fit for the task of coaching kids.

Isn't there a way of screening prospective coaches so we can reduce the odds of getting stuck with a problem personality?

Someday, there may be a psychological profile that will be used to filter out the bad candidates. But for now, we have to rely on other, less formal measures of aptitudes and attitudes.

I recommend a gradual, behavioral approach to selecting coaches. Let's say a child is about to play soccer for her first year. During that period, most parents would be happy to watch from the sidelines and not attempt to coach. But there are exceptions.

Those who want to coach without having ever done so might be screened for suitable experience with kids—apart from parenting. For instance, an elementary school teacher might be given a chance, but a middle manager with a strictly business background wouldn't merit the same priority of consideration. The latter would be asked to gradually work his or her way through the ranks.

Here's how the process could work, using the example of a willing, eager, but inexperienced father:

1. At first, he could assist the regular coaches. If they needed someone to help out with drills during practices, he might lend a hand. This would give him contact with the players, but he'd be supervised at all times by the regular staff.

2. The following season, he might be appointed as one of two, or

possibly three, assistant coaches. Being a junior coach, he'd be given increasing responsibilities during the season. For instance, he and the more senior assistant might be asked to conduct a practice or two in the absence of the head coach. As the season drew to a close, this pair might be responsible for coaching the team by themselves during an entire game or two.

3. During the third year, he would be elevated to the status of second-level assistant coach. He'd be the acting head coach in the absence of the formal head coach. He could have substantial input into strategic decisions regarding which players are to be assigned to certain positions. In any emergency in which the head coach could no longer serve, the second in command could take over, with a minimum of fuss or disruption.

4. During his fourth year, he might be given a team of his own, as head coach. Among his duties would be the cultivation of future coaches, in the same way that he was brought along—slowly but surely.

Because I've coached three different sports, my coaching skills have been developed on three different tracks. In soccer, I was a parent-helper and then an assistant coach. Occasionally, I'd be responsible for running practices and coaching games.

In basketball, I was one of two assistants, but because my associates were often absent, I was asked to run the entire show on a number of occasions. This wasn't nearly as comfortable as coming through the ranks gradually.

In baseball, I was a parent-helper for a few years, and then I was asked to manage a team. My choice was to be an assistant coach first, but the league insisted it needed a manager, so I accepted the job. Of all of my experiences, this was the most abrupt, and the least satisfying.

Going from relative outsider to chief was quite a leap, and it put me in the position of having to learn a lot of details very quickly. Had I served as an assistant, I could have learned these particulars over a few years.

The great advantage to coming through the ranks gradually is that you get to learn at a comfortable rate, and parents and fellow coaches can get acquainted with you in a relaxed manner. Your skills will be visible, and you'll be able to assess whether coaching is really a good fit for you and for your family.

You might consider this sequence of involvement as providing a three-year apprenticeship for prospective head coaches. This should be plenty of time to screen out those who aren't going to make a meaningful contribution to the kids, and to their leagues.

23.

Should Nonparents Be Coaches?

MOST OF THE coaches you'll encounter in kids' sports will be the players' moms and dads, but every now and then, you'll come across a volunteer coach who doesn't have a child on the team. In fact, some may not be parents at all.

When I was growing up, our Little League had a coach who was a big hit with the kids, though he was single and childless. Just beyond college age, Buddy was an energetic fellow who looked like Thor from the comic books—except he had a buzz haircut. He coached the Cubs with intensity but also with an easygoing sense of humor.

Everybody seemed to like him, and when I had a chance to interact with him on all-star teams, I was impressed by how much he knew about the sport. Later, in other leagues, it became more commonplace for nonparents to volunteer as coaches because they loved the sport as well as the challenge of developing young players. At those levels, being a parent wasn't a prerequisite for leadership.

In Little League, however, it was rare to see nonparents as coaches or managers. There are arguments for allowing them as well as for disallowing them.

Because they don't have kids on the team, they shouldn't have to face as many conflicts of interest or claims of favoritism when it comes to assigning positions. In addition, since they're somewhat detached from the passions of parenthood, they might be slightly more objective in evaluating the skills of their players. Plus, the league in which they're involved may not take them for granted nearly as much as it does coaches who can be expected to hang around for years as their kids move through the ranks.

On the other hand, when coaches are parents, they're stakeholders in the same schools and neighborhoods as the rest of the parents and players. This can contribute to greater cohesiveness and to a greater sense of responsibility to respond to the sentiments of the fans and families. It may also promote participation by a broader range of parents when they feel that their team is in the hands of an insider rather than an outsider.

I suppose there is another reason to support having parents be coaches. They strike many of us as being safer, in the sense that they know what it's like to love children and want to protect them in the special ways that parents do, from the moment they're born. Others, no matter how noble and pure of heart, may not feel that special pain that a parent feels when his or her child gets a scrape or a cut. They may not have the depth of experience with kids, in sickness and in health, to properly decode a player's statement "I'm tired" as meaning that the child is really ill and is not just making conversation or an excuse.

Despite these potential minuses, Coach Buddy was nice to have around, even if you were on an opposing team. He looked like the sort of athlete many of us hoped we'd become one day.

He also brought a sense of baseball professionalism to our games. No parent of my childhood had the sort of energy and quick reflexes Buddy had. Yet, for all of his strengths, his teams fared no better than others in the standings—which were led by guys who showed up to practices in slacks and ties instead of sweats.

So, if the issue ever comes up, and a nonparent like Buddy wants to coach, I hope you'll give the candidate a tryout. The kids might really appreciate having a "buddy" of their own around.

24.

Selecting the Right Team Parent

IF YOU WANT to have a smoothly running team, you'll need to select the right kind of team parent. This is the person who is generally in charge of "communications."

Specifically:

1. This volunteer will be the message center for the inbound calls of parents. Did the coaches call an extra practice during spring break? The team parent will have the answer to this question.

If a child has an important music recital and will miss the next two games, the team parent will be informed and will, in turn, tell the coaches.

2. He or she will coordinate snack schedules. For a parent who is wondering whether it's her turn to bring goodies next week or the following week, the team parent is the one with the master schedule.

3. The team parent will distribute all written communications from the league or the coaches. If there is a special clinic to be held on the topic of bunting, the team parent will get the word out—usually through a flyer, if there is enough time.

4. The team parent will make calls to remind parents of upcoming practices and games.

5. If special orders need to be placed for optional purchases, such as team jackets, the team parent will be in charge of collecting the money and coordinating the order with the vendor.

6. If other parents are needed for scoring games or serving as referees, the team parent will recruit them and schedule their participation.

7. The team parent will also coordinate the ordering of trophies.

8. Finally, the team parent takes responsibility for arranging the end-of-the-season party.

That's a pretty long list, isn't it? You can see at a glance how important the team parent function is. This person is like the head administrator of the team. If he or she slips up, your team's functioning will be greatly impaired.

That said, what should you be looking for in a team parent? Here are a few suggestions:

- It helps a lot if the team parent has had some experience in this kind of role. Experienced people will have gone through the cycle of an entire season, and they'll know how to get things done. They won't have to invent an entirely new routine.

- Having assisted another team parent is the next best preparation for doing the job.

- If you're faced with candidates who are all novices, I suggest you select one who has a lot of spare time to devote to the task. Often, this will mean an individual who does not have a full-time job.

- A working parent who volunteers may be very suitable, providing he or she is accessible and doesn't have to travel out of town too often.

- Select someone who seems to be a good communicator. Someone who makes other parents feel defensive will only hurt the cohesiveness of your team.

- Recruit an assistant for the new team parent who will be given real responsibilities. Ideally, the assistant will be a person with a young child on the team and thus able to move up later into a full-fledged team parent.

- Choose someone with whom you can comfortably interact. The right sort of person will not only perform the duties mentioned but also be your link to the parents. How are they feeling about the team? Are their kids feeling good about the experience?

A good team parent will be attuned to these issues, and will keep you continuously informed.

So, choose wisely.

PART IV

Coaching Your Players

25.

Why You Can't Effectively Coach Your Own Kid

A SAVVY YMCA basketball trainer informed his new class of eager parent-coaches, "I could tell my boy something a hundred times, and he simply won't get it. But along comes another coach who offers the same tip once, and my kid thinks it's brilliant, and he immediately puts it to work! It always happens that way."

You've probably heard the expression "No one is a prophet in his or her own land." Well, the same wisdom applies to coaching one's own kids. It's nearly impossible for your kids to think you're a gift to coaching. They know you too well. As another oft-heard adage explains, "Familiarity breeds contempt."

Our kids discount much of what we tell them. Partly, this is because we're constantly telling them so much about so many things that the relative value of another tidbit of information—even if it pertains to sports—seems insignificant.

Unless you're Mark McGwire, and your boy hands out bats for the St. Louis Cardinals, your kid probably won't think you know a thing about sports. That's because *you're old*! (At least, in his or her eyes.)

You don't make your living by coaching, so how could you know anything? Oh, that's right. You played ball in school and you set records in Little League. Hey, that was in the prehistoric era, wasn't it? Weren't dinosaurs grazing in the outfield while you played? How could anything from that epoch apply to this enlightened, modern era?

If you are one of a number of coaches on a team, take it upon yourself to let the others know that they can't effectively coach their kids either. This will spare them and their offspring a lot of frustration and wasted energy. Then, make a pact to take responsibility for paying special attention to each other's kids.

If you have a tip that you simply must deliver to a player who is in your immediate family, act like a ventriloquist. Don't even bother telling the child what to do. Instead, have your words come from the lips of a fellow coach.

You still won't seem like a prophet, but at least your "brilliance" won't fall on deaf ears.

26.

Make Your "Plodders" Feel Special

YOU'RE BOUND TO have at least two or three players who don't stand out. They'll quietly perform the drills, play their positions without fanfare or distinction, and have only occasional moments of glory.

If they were members of a theatrical troupe, they'd be cast as the spear-carriers, or their voices would be hidden in a chorus; they'd never be awarded the leads or the solos. Nevertheless, without these troupers, you couldn't have an ensemble performance.

In sports, they're the ones I affectionately refer to as the plodders. Reminiscent of "The Tortoise and the Hare," they seem destined to inch their way along without a care in the world while others run by. But plodders need to be made to feel like winners as well.

Our task isn't to push these solid but average performers beyond their limits. It is to enable them to have as much fun as they can possibly have, and to feel as important to our teams as they actually are.

How can you do this? Several ways:

- During practices, make a big deal out of their small improvements. They won't go from kicking thin air to kicking goal after goal in soccer, but they may go from kicking the air to kicking the ball. That's your chance to exclaim, "Good contact, Lauren!" Hearing this, she'll be motivated to consolidate her gains and improve even more.

- When you're together on the sidelines, or during halftime, ask your plodders how they're doing. Discover what they think of the game so far. This question alone and the fact that you're paying attention to them will improve the quality of their sports experience.

- After games, make sure to acknowledge their contributions as you talk with your team. What if nothing remarkable happened at third base? Say "I could see you were really ready over there at all times, even though there wasn't much action. Good concentration, Mike!"

- Periodically, give them a new perspective on the game by trying them at a different position. It might mean a slight move from left forward to right forward, or from left field to center, but it will break the monotony. Again, by paying attention to them, you add to their enjoyment.

Children develop at different rates. We all know this, if only by observing our kids' friends; some shoot up several inches during a summer, while others seem to take more time. The same thing applies to playing abilities.

Today's plodders may become tomorrow's all-stars, providing they feel good enough about their sports experiences to stick with the sport. Even if they never experience an athletic breakthrough, they can still have a lot of fun and can come to appreciate their many contributions.

27.

Handling the "Prima Donna"

IT'S ALSO ALMOST inevitable that every season or two, you'll be both blessed and cursed by having a standout player on your team.

The good news is that kids like this will be able to play nearly any position with ease and grace. In fact, their exploits will seem to make the other players all but disappear the moment games begin.

The bad news is that such abilities can go to one's head. Instead of being even slightly modest, the standout will exhibit arrogance and impatience with the "inferior" playing abilities of his or her peers, and will even want to do your coaching for you.

The prima donnas will openly complain about your drills in practice. They'll tell their peers how to play their positions and will be bossy and tactless in critiquing them.

In a word, these standout athletes with oversize egos can be a pain. When you try to give them tips, they and their parents glare at you. The unspoken message from Mom and Dad is "Leave her alone; she's perfect—*you're* not going to improve her!"

What can you do to make potential prima donnas easier to take? Here's my approach:

1. Avoid allowing the development of a "star system"—a tacit agreement that there are separate rules for special people. For instance, they can't be allowed to arrive late to practices or games and still qualify for the starting lineup. They may throw a tantrum for being disciplined. Your team could score fewer goals, points, or runs, and even lose, as a result. But that's life.

2. Work your you-know-what off to develop a second or third "star" to deflect attention from number one. Through their improvement, you'll

send an important message that talents are distributed and that you're not relying on only one player to carry the team.

Seeing others improve, prima donna types may start to push themselves to regain their slipping stature. They'll push themselves instead of others and become better teammates because of the competition.

3. Develop a player, or even two players, who can play the favorite position of the star. Then, when they're up to speed, rotate them into that slot. This will send a message that no one is irreplaceable.

All three of these steps are methods of asserting control as a coach, which is a fundamental requirement if you're going to succeed. At the same time, each one is also a solid way of improving the cohesiveness as well as the playing abilities of your entire team.

28.

Kids Who Don't Have or Can't Afford the Equipment

I DIDN'T HAVE to coach girls' softball for long to notice an unusual sort of discrimination with which a few of my players had to contend. Many of their parents hesitated to provide them with the same quality of equipment that their brothers were given.

For instance, girls were expected to catch eleven-inch softballs with gloves barely larger than their hands. When I mentioned to them that they needed larger mitts, they just looked down at the turf and shook their heads.

One of them lamented, "My dad will never buy me a new glove. He won't buy me anything!" She wasn't exaggerating by much. In fact, some girls aren't provided with sliding pads. These are essential skin coverings that enable girls to safely slide into bases. If they aren't wearing pads, they'll either not slide, and get thrown out or collide with opponents, or slide and probably scrape and cut up their legs.

By denying their daughters sliding pads, parents prevented them from playing the game as it was designed. Moreover, they precluded me from coaching properly. I'd hesitate to instruct these players to slide when situations called for it.

I noticed that some of these same parents had sons who showed up for their games and practices in complete uniforms. They seemed to have the best of everything, including sufficiently large gloves. Why were boys deserving of the proper equipment while girls were left to fend without the basics?

I decided to lay down the law. I started telling offending parents, "I can't play your daughter if she doesn't have the right equipment, like sliding pads." Usually, by the following game, these girls were completely

suited up, and then they became effective base runners and base stealers—to the surprise and delight of their folks.

If you coach, make sure your players get the right equipment. If they
don't, ask their parents to get on the stick. Don't accept excuses, and don't
allow a double standard to persist if you see it, where girls are treated one
way and boys another.

If cost is the issue, ask your league to chip in from the general fund
to ensure that everyone has the right gear.

29.

"But I'm Really *Trying*!"

WHEN I WAS a college professor, I frequently graded papers and oral presentations. One part of this process that I dreaded was dealing with the kids who felt they deserved a higher mark than the one they received.

I could justify their scores, but what was difficult was rebutting their belief that a better mark should have been awarded because they spent a lot of time on their projects and they "tried hard."

"Isn't effort *worth* something?" is a question I'd often hear. I'd respond with my standard minilecture: "Yes, effort is worth a lot because true achievement is less likely to occur without it. But I'm not here to assess effort, because I can't *see* it. You do that at home or in the library or within the confines of your mind. I can only see the *product* of your efforts. If the product is a C, then an A's worth of effort won't change that result."

The impassioned counterclaim would be: "But I know for a fact that Jean just whipped together *her* report, and *she* got a B. That's not fair!"

After providing as much corrective feedback about the project as I could, I'd end the debate with: "Keep trying, and your work will improve. Then, your grades will reflect your effort."

I thought this type of discussion was behind me, until I got into coaching and kids asked to be assigned to certain positions in the batting lineup or on the field. One player continually pestered me about playing second base. Unfortunately, she wasn't skilled enough to become a starter at that position.

Once or twice, I gave her a shot at playing second, but I regretted it because she quickly treated that assignment as an entitlement. After being replaced, she'd ask, "Why can't I stay there? I'm really trying hard!"

There it was, again—that old claim—but I couldn't give this eleven-year-old an abstract lecture about "effort versus results." I couldn't tell her that the two infielders who were better at the position seemed to have more natural ability, and therefore, they didn't have to try nearly as hard. Like being in a state of athletic grace, they could simply float from play to play, making tough moves seem routine.

Kids who aren't "naturals" at a given sport always have to try harder. It's probably the same way with mathematics and with public speaking. Gifted mathematicians are said to "intuit" the answers to difficult problems. Allegedly, they work them out in their heads. Great speakers often have the "gift of gab," feeling completely at ease in front of groups. By comparison, others struggle.

The struggling player presents a special challenge.

We want kids to work hard—even the so-called naturals. By no means do we want to punish someone's efforts, even if they aren't bearing immediate fruit. **So, what can we do to keep hardworking underachievers motivated?**

Try to analyze their shortcomings while devising specific drills for them to practice. I helped my would-be second-base player by having everyone field more fly balls and hard-hit grounders. During the drills, she could see that she missed more balls than the two girls who were being regularly platooned in the position. Without fanfare, this gave them credibility while showing her, quite graphically, what she needed to do to improve.

I showed her how to practice by herself between games. Armed with an improvement plan, she'd have less time to complain about unfairness. She could invest her energy in doing specific things that would improve her skills.

Trying hard doesn't always lead to demonstrable improvement. But it is so important, in so many areas of life, that it is worth rewarding if we can find a way to do it—especially when kids are young. By the time they reach college, we can only hope that it will be a good habit and that it will be enjoyed for the intrinsic satisfaction it can bring.

30.

Coaching the Youngest
and the Smallest

ALMOST EVERY TEAM has a player who seems especially young for his or her age, or who is physically smaller than other players. It's tempting to start making up special rules to accommodate this player.

After all, this child may have been the last one chosen in the draft and has had no other experience playing a team sport. Compared with the rest of the players on the team, this one seems a little disoriented, and possibly a little shy. You sense that if you don't pay special attention to such cases, they'll get lost in the shuffle.

But I have good news for you. I've never coached a team on which there wasn't a "small-fry" who distinguished himself or herself on the court or playing field.

How can this be, you might wonder, when their physical stature and tender years make them appear so vulnerable and weak compared with their peers?

I explain it a few ways. First, their parents must realize that their offspring are somewhat more diminutive than their buddies, yet they have signed them up for a sport anyway. Generally, this signifies that the parent has a certain degree of faith and courage, and these attitudes are being communicated to and embodied by the child.

I've also seen players who you assume will excel turn out to be mediocre. A few years ago, our soccer team had a girl who seemed, by birth, to be equipped perfectly for the game. Long-limbed, she could stride across the field with ease. Her coordination was super, and nature seemed to have endowed her with excellent balance. She towered over her teammates, who initially felt intimidated—until they got to know her better.

I assumed this player would help us make it to the play-offs. I also figured she could probably look forward to a great future in athletics. Yet, despite her physical advantages, she was afraid of kicking the ball and hurting others—and, for that matter, of being kicked. She seemed to have difficulty visualizing success on the playing field, so she never lived up to her apparent promise as an athlete. Though she was urged by her coaches to play more aggressively, she didn't rise to the occasion.

There is another reason small kids do well. They size up the competition and realize, consciously or unconsciously, that they're going to have to try harder to generate results. I've seen wee ones throw themselves in front of balls to block shots, when their taller peers would shudder at the thought.

Moreover, there are positions in many sports in which smaller stature may confer benefits. Someone who is small but speedy may be a perfect leadoff hitter and base stealer. Last season, we placed a small but exceedingly quick soccer player on defense, figuring she could deflect balls before our goalie had to touch them. The strategy paid off: we won the knockout tournament, and our smallest and youngest player made the all-star team.

So, don't sell these athletes short. They may "come up big" by the end of the season.

31.

Team Clowns: Pluses and Minuses

IF YOU READ the sports pages, it's a cinch you'll come across a writer who feels that a slumping pro team keeps losing because it lacks "chemistry." Chemistry isn't what hits balls out of the park for home runs. It doesn't give a pitcher the arm of a Kevin Brown or a Pedro Martinez.

But it makes team play a lot more fun. I suppose you could define *chemistry* as the personality that a team takes on because it has certain people on the roster.

Some players will be utterly serious and focused. Others will seem scatterbrained and only loosely connected to the here and now. And one person, the team clown, may be the jokester or prankster who keeps everyone else loose and laughing.

Clowns can be helpful or hurtful to your team, depending upon how you treat them.

When people speak of the 1988 World Champion Los Angeles Dodgers, they often note that Mickey Hatcher was the team clown. His lightheartedness as well as on-the-field enthusiasm reportedly helped the club to become winners.

You may have a team clown as well. If you do, I hope you'll take special care of this person. Such a player may seem like an irritant, someone who pops off just as you're imparting your best lesson about rebounding, but be patient. He or she could be the safety valve you need to keep winning or losing pressures in perspective and under control.

I had a team clown who went overboard. She joked way too much, and I had to rein her in. But, after analyzing her abilities, I determined that her skills were misplaced. Instead of putting her in in the outfield, I gave her a try at third base.

She made three great plays, which helped us to win the game. After that, she settled down and seemed to get serious about baseball. We lost a clown but gained a better player.

Try something new with your team clowns. Give them more responsibilities, and take the entire spectrum of their talents seriously.

They may stop laughing long enough to start smiling on the inside. And they may give you yet another way to win.

32.

Managing the Other Coaches' Kids

AT THE BEGINNING of this section, I explained why you can't effectively coach your own kid. I also mentioned that they can be effectively guided by your fellow coaches.

This means you bear the primary responsibility for coaching the kids of your fellow coaches.

As you might imagine, this is easier said than done. Here are some common traps in which you can get snared:

- You might assume that the parents have already given them the guidance they need.

- You might assume that the parents will resent the advice you give to their kids—especially if it contradicts the parent's own suggestions.

- You may pamper the kids because the parents won't, to avoid the appearance of playing favorites.

- You may give them choice assignments and the "best" positions as a form of acknowledgment of the hard work of the parents as coaches.

- You may go overboard in the other direction and be too tough on them—expecting too much from their performance on the field.

Here's what I suggest. Do your best to take a fresh look at each child's capabilities and limitations. It's likely that the coach-parent is not perceiving the child objectively, and you have a better perspective. Take advantage of this role distance to try the player out at new positions.

Give your coaches' kids a chance to have as wide a spectrum of experiences as those to which other players will be exposed. That way, you'll provide them with an enjoyable sports experience.

Your efforts should be handsomely rewarded because your fellow coaches will be doing the same thing for your child.

33.

Coaching the Nonalert

You'll find it's especially challenging to coach a child who isn't alert.

Nonalert kids put themselves and others in danger because they suddenly space out in the middle of games or even in the middle of plays. On one of my teams, I had a third-base player who was one of these space cadets.

Here's what would happen. The catcher would see that a runner was taking too big a lead off the bag. She'd pivot and throw, and our player, instead of anticipating this move, would be lost in a fog. The ball would whistle past her face, missing it by a fraction of an inch.

As a coach, you can't let this type of player constitute a danger to herself or others.

How could her detachment threaten others? Take the same pickoff play. Instead of throwing the ball at eye level, the catcher aims it lower. Its trajectory will impact the returning player at the base of the neck—unless the third-base player gets her glove on it.

If she's daydreaming, she'll let the ball fly, unfettered and undeflected. And then we might have a tragedy on our hands.

We can expect the attention spans of even average, "normal" kids to be fairly short. We should *expect* them to tune out, but we need to be there to snap them back to attention.

This means you need to be prepared to be a bit of a "shouter." If a ball is flying to my third-base player, I'm going to let her know, in a loud and quick way. So should you. Don't worry about seeming too loud. You can't be when dealing with the nonalert.

34.
Key Issues in Coaching Girls and Boys

A GROWING LITERATURE in the social and behavioral sciences points to the fact that girls and boys learn differently. Just as their bodies operate on different timetables, so do their minds.

There's one finding that I think is most pertinent to coaching: **Girls seem to be more afraid of making mistakes than boys.**

For instance, if you ask girls to take certain sports risks—such as deciding whether to steal a base or to stay where they are—they'll tend to "freeze up" more often than boys will in the same situation. Instead of risking being caught stealing, and therefore feeling that they made the wrong decision, they may opt for the more conservative, risk-averse alternative of staying put.

According to research cited by author (*How Girls Thrive*) and educator JoAnn Deak, Ph.D., girls react differently than boys in certain competitive situations. In a speech before the Westridge School for girls in Pasadena, California, in October 1998, Dr. Deak said that girls are more likely to *hesitate* before taking action. Proof of this hesitation phenomenon is seen in competitive academic events. These "Decathlons" are like the old *College Bowl* television program. Two teams square off at opposing tables; the moderator asks a question, and the respondent quickest in hitting the buzzer gets the first chance to answer.

Dr. Deak noted a recurring problem with a team from an all-girls school. They would answer far fewer questions than boys would. As you can imagine, this decreased their odds of winning tremendously.

When asked about this, they said they frequently knew the answers but hesitated. Further exploration revealed that they were so afraid of the stigma of being wrong in a "public" setting that they stopped themselves from striking their buzzers.

Were they just as smart as their male counterparts, if not smarter? Absolutely, yet they couldn't win unless they could learn to hit their buzzers without second-guessing themselves.

Their school did something imaginative to help them to overcome this problem. They brought in a coach. The coach's task wasn't to help the team to cram for the event, though. It was to help them to perform only one task: to hear a question and then race to hit their buzzers.

Coaching helped. The girls' team started winning the race to the buzzer, earning those fleeting chances to showcase what they really knew all along.

I have coached girls who are every bit as aggressive and unhesitating as boys—at least in some areas. For instance, in softball, one of my most talented catchers was an avid base runner; she loved doing delayed steals. She'd wait until the split second when the opposing catcher would throw the ball back to the pitcher. This is a gutsy move, especially when you're stealing home. She seemed to thrive on the excitement of these plays, despite the fact that she'd get thrown out every now and then.

Here's the curious part. As a catcher, she had a rifle arm and was capable of gunning down more base stealers than any other catcher in the league. But *this* was when she hesitated. Although she'd have a clear chance to erase a runner from the base paths, she'd wait too long to let go of the ball.

The same thing would apply to pickoff plays. When she had a taunting runner who jumped to a big lead from first or third, she'd wait until the player turned back toward the base to let go of the ball.

Countless times, I suggested: "Catch them when they're leaning toward the next base. That way, they'll twist themselves into pretzels to get back, and you'll nab them!"

Did she have the arm strength and accuracy and aggressiveness to do this? Unquestionably, but her problem was in second-guessing her first and better impulse. Only by telling her that I didn't care if she threw the ball away—that I wanted her to practice, even during games—did I get her to "pull the trigger" more often and on time.

In other words, she had to learn to get to the buzzer.

I applied this principle to all of my players. I'd have everyone, including the slowest, stealing bases. My goal was to relieve them of the fear that they'd fail. I told them, "If I give you the steal sign, and they throw you out, it's my fault, not yours. Blame me. If you make it, though, it'll be because you earned it."

It seemed to work. Our team was the most aggressive in our league. But fighting the impulse to hesitate is a never-ending battle.

As research tells us more about gender, we can refine and improve our coaching. Coaches shouldn't hesitate to use any tool that will improve performance and enjoyment.

35.

Coaching the Kid Who Shouldn't Be There

ALMOST EVERY TEAM has one.

They're the kids who don't pay attention when you're trying to demonstrate bunting techniques. They tend to make jokes at inopportune times, diverting the attention of the other players. They have much less natural playing ability than your other players. They're kids who shouldn't really be there.

You'll know who they are because you'll ask yourself why they *are* there, and you won't generate a good reason. Yet, there is one.

They are on your team because their parents are making them play. When children are compelled in this way, the sport no longer feels like "play." It's more like forced labor, and kids resent it, unless they find other compensations.

As a coach, what can you do for the kid who shouldn't be there?

First of all, don't succumb to the temptation to write the child off. A player who is making any effort whatsoever has *some* potential for improvement. Your challenge is to bring out this kid's best in the most pleasant way you can under the circumstances.

Try using compliments. Be shamelessly upbeat when it comes to lavishing praise on your players—and especially on the less developed ones.

Try to generate at least one drill through which the child can excel. For example, to warm up, I had my softball players take a few laps around the field; then, I had them sprint for speed. I was pleased to see that Toni, one of my reluctant players, was really quick. I had never noticed this. I ran alongside of her, and when we finished toward the head of the pack, I exclaimed, "Great running, Toni! You are *quick*! Whoa!"

She beamed, and she became one of our most spirited and accomplished base runners. Because of her speed, I was able to elevate her in the batting order, with confidence that she could score from nearly any base.

Having found a constructive role for herself, she was no longer a distraction. Instead of being sullen and listless, she showed the kind of energy and interest every player should exhibit.

So, try to find the hidden talents in players who seem to be on the team only reluctantly. They'll often come to life and start to really enjoy the experience.

36.

Coaching Your Innate Leaders

HAVE YOU EVER noticed that certain kids seem to magnetically attract their peers? They're the ones who are sought out more than others in their age-group, and even kids who are younger or older think they're "cool."

It may be hard for an adult to understand these attractions, but they occur. Inevitably, you're going to have one player who will exude charisma. These are the natural born leaders, if only because others will blissfully follow them. You'll want to make sure yours is a constructive influence.

Take Mary, for example. She played on one of my soccer teams. A bundle of energy, she seemed to generate a "following" from the first time we assembled as a team to practice.

She didn't have any extra abilities or skills to go with her other charms; she was just herself, and that was enough to transform her into a veritable pied piper. If she got carried away cracking jokes, other players would giggle and guffaw their way through entire practices and games. When she led a cheer, they also cheered like there was no tomorrow.

An innate leader can help your team or hurt it, depending on the child's mood or whims. That's why we need to recognize the power that such a player has and do whatever we can to make sure it is used constructively.

One of the best ways to accomplish this is by "deputizing" this player to do certain things. For example, you might ask him or her to keep an eye on the team's equipment during practices or games. Or, the assignment can be to count the number of times players make contact during batting practice, in order to assure that everyone gets a turn.

In other words, the best way to prevent your innate leaders from going bad is to give them constructive responsibilities.

That said, we also need to praise them for their help. Without positive reinforcement, they'll see no reason to help out and may even be tempted to turn to "The Dark Side of the Force."

How can you tell who your innate leader is? Just observe your kids when they're taking a water or refreshment break. Who seems to attract a small crowd of peers? That's the one.

By the way, your innate leaders could be great players. That would be beneficial because their teammates will naturally want to emulate them. But leaders could as easily have average or even below-average athletic skills. In Mary's case, I didn't want the others emulating her, at least when it came to their level of play.

When your innate leaders aren't great athletes, it becomes even more important for you to give them extra roles to play so that they'll use their charisma for constructive ends. When you do this, you'll find that you have to invest much less energy riding herd on them.

Then, you can take the team where you, the *formal* leader, want it to go!

37.

Coaching the Listless

EVERY NOW AND then, you'll face the challenge of coaching kids who do nearly everything at a snail's pace.

Some are simply showing how tired they feel by the time they reach practices or games. Given the increasing tendency of today's parents to overschedule their offspring, booking them into countless after-school programs, it's no wonder some players seem to be dragging.

Occasionally, I suspect a lethargic demeanor is a smoke screen that covers up other issues. For example, a sluggish-seeming kid may not feel secure when playing a given sport. Feeling less than fully capable, the child might take on a detached, "I'm-not-really-trying" attitude. This can help the child to rationalize future failings.

Or, such kids could be angry with a parent for sticking them into this sport when they really wanted to have time to play with their pals after school.

Possibly, a player who seems listless is upset with you for assigning him or her to a least-favored playing position.

In short, any number of things could be going on. No matter the cause, I suggest the same remedies:

- Pay attention to the child, and smile. Make such players feel welcome.

- Use the child's name. Perhaps more than others, these kids need to feel that they're important, and that they're *visible* to you.

- Make small talk, and ask them how they're doing.

- If you warm up with your players by sprinting on the court or by running laps around the field, buddy up with your listless player. Run next to him or her. Every now and then, challenge the kid to a friendly race. (Let the player beat you!)

- Assign listless kids to playing positions where they're bound to get a lot of action, and where they'll find it hard to doze off. Try them at center in basketball, at first base in softball, or at a forward position in soccer. Avoid banishing a player like this to any position where there are long pauses between events, as there are in the outfield or at goalie.

Treat your listless players as if they are shy guests at a party. They may just need some encouragement to get their motors running. Once you get them into the habit of acting exuberantly, they'll tend to keep doing it without further prodding.

38.

Coaching the "All-Star"

I'LL BET THAT you're going to start your coaching career with a team having at least one player of all-star caliber. All-stars' level of play is clearly superior to that of their peers. And they know it.

So do their teammates and every parent and coach in the league. These are elite, young athletes who, a few years ago, couldn't be counted on to tie their own shoes, let alone tie the score with a dramatic shot at the final buzzer.

They may be so good that they're being scouted by higher leagues. They could even have an "aura," or a body bubble, that makes them seem taller and more muscular than they are. In a sense, they're already celebrities.

But like many things, they can be at once an opportunity and a danger. If you handle them well, they can fulfill their promise and achieve for your team and for themselves; mishandled, they can cause calamity.

A delicate situation arises when you feel you have to discipline them. Let's say they're perennially late to or absent from practices.

In any sport, you'd be justified in benching the player at the beginning of the next scheduled game. If you do, however, your action won't go unnoticed. Every parent and other coach in the league will see what has happened, and they'll have an opinion about the move you made.

Some kids and parents will claim that you're punishing the whole team by withholding your all-star from any part of a contest. They'll say you're reducing the ability of the team to play as competitively as it can, or even dooming it to lose.

As other teams take advantage of the all-star's benching, you'll second-guess yourself about your decision to sanction the player. His or her replacement will make a serious error that the superstar might have handled routinely. You'll groan inside, while those in the bleachers won't hold back. You'll hear their groans of disappointment. So, what can you do?

I'd stay the course and privately explain to the player that he or she is important to the team but has to play by the same rules as everybody else. I'd explain that great players are role models, like it or not.

Accordingly, they bear a special burden. Other kids look up to them and try to mirror what they do—both the good and the bad—and want to act the same way. Unless a sanction is doled out, the other players will mistakenly believe that it's OK for them to miss practices as well. Then, the skills of the entire team will degrade.

Apart from disciplining your all-star, there's something even more crucial and challenging that you should do. You should try to create a second and, if possible, a third player of all-star caliber.

Don't rely exclusively on your best player to bear the burden of delivering outstanding results. If one kid is clearly better than everyone else on the team, you can expect that player to engage you in a battle of wills or a big showdown sooner or later.

Kids do this with all authority figures. It's just a part of growing up. But while they're rebelling, your second and third all-stars can help to carry the team.

A player of all-star quality presents advantages and disadvantages. Optimize your team's results by doing everything you can to augment the skills of everyone else.

39.

What If Your Kid Is Having a Lousy Time?

IF YOU'RE A coach's kid, there's a lot of pressure placed on your shoulders.

First of all, you're presumed to be a reflection of Mom's or Dad's athleticism—so, parents and peers expect you to be a cut above other players your age. Second, you're a role model, so you can't goof off in practices or during games—at least not as much as others. Third, you travel with the coach, so you're required to arrive earlier, depart later, and carry a bunch of stuff. In other words, you're not just a player; you're also a worker. Fourth, other kids may want to use you to send messages to the coach, such as "I want to be a forward and not a guard."

All of these burdens can get to be too much for certain kids. Unlike the run-of-the-mill player, your kid can't quietly quit the team, or take some mental-health days off, without it reflecting negatively on you. If he or she is having a bad season, this fact can also make you feel miserable.

What can you do if kids are burning out? I think the best thing to do is relieve them of some of the pressure. First, try to remember that they're kids and not junior adults or future coaches. They're there to have fun, first and foremost. When the fun stops, they'll probably grind to a halt.

Second, it's helpful to have someone else transport them to the gym or to the field. Your spouse may be a good candidate for this labor of love. If that isn't possible, develop a car pool. This will give your kid some valuable socializing time with teammates, outside of your sphere of influence. For a precious half hour or so, your child will be offstage. And peers can see that he or she is just a nice kid who happens to have a coach as a parent.

If your kid is going through a slump, don't jump in to fix everything—at least not without an invitation. I'd broach the subject this way:

"If you'd like some shooting tips, I'm sure Coach Shirley would be happy to give you some. Or, I will. Just let me know, ok?"

It's hard to accept sports pointers from a parent, particularly if the parent is a coach. So, tread lightly here, and your kid will have more fun. Generally, if your kid seems to be having a lousy time, it will pass before too long, if you don't become overbearing.

PART V

Managing the Parents

40.

Moms and Dads View
Sports Differently

IF YOU WERE to ask me how sports benefit kids, I'd say that sports do nothing less than help to prepare them for adulthood.

Specifically, sports teach kids to compete, cooperate with teammates, overcome adversity, follow directions, and develop leadership capabilities.

My wife, on the other hand, says sports give kids a chance to make new friends, provide healthy outlets for pent-up energies, teach kids about the meaning of "fair play," help kids to become well rounded, and give Mom a chance to commune with other parents.

Of course, sports can do all of these things, but the focus seems to shift, depending on whether women or men are running the show as coaches.

For instance, the other evening, my wife and I attended an organizational meeting for this season's soccer team. I've elected to give my daughter a break from Coach Dad and simply be another parent, cheering from the sidelines.

The head coach is a mom with vast experience. First, she gave a nice speech to the players, emphasizing teamwork and fair play. She mentioned that winning and losing aren't as important as having fun and playing like a team. She also stated, "There won't be any stars on this team—everyone will be treated the same way." This suggested to me that she wants to nip in the bud any destructive, intrateam competition.

She then invited her assistant, a dad, to say a few words. He wasn't nearly as succinct because he seemed to be avoiding saying certain things directly. He spent a lot of time talking about the "commitment" that players must demonstrate.

Then, he started to sound like a dour taskmaster. He stated the necessity of "giving 100 percent on the playing field" and that "there won't be any players who will be able to get away with half efforts." He predicted that our team would look much more solid than any other that we'd encounter, and that our practices would be run very efficiently.

Although he didn't directly contradict anything the head coach said, it was clear from his tone and language that he was a driver, and that this team was going to *compete*. He expected to win, and he wasn't going to accept any excuses.

As the meeting concluded, my wife and I chatted with some parents whom we've known from a number of other sports. They shared my impression that we had just been exposed to two differing and, to an extent, mutually exclusive coaching philosophies.

I took the opportunity to ask them what they thought of the Y-Winners basketball program, in which the other dad and I had recently coached. I was especially interested in what they thought about the fact that games weren't scored.

The mom was ecstatic. She said she thought the experience was great. As she spoke, I monitored the fidgeting of the dad. It was clear that he wasn't nearly as sold on the idea of not knowing which team was ahead. Apparently, he was someone who liked clearcut victories.

As our chat continued, I could see that the dad and mom had quite different aspirations for their kids when they played sports. He wanted them to compete and to improve their skills. Just having fun, socializing, and exercising weren't enough.

Mom was happy if her daughters were learning, but her real thrill was seeing that her kids had a pleasant overall experience from participating. She sounded protective—not wanting them to be pushed or to be pressured by coaches. The dad, on the other hand, wanted them out there making names for themselves. If they had to be pushed a little, so be it.

I'm convinced that moms and dads foster differing views of sports, and there's nothing wrong with this. Perhaps we can respect these differences as a system of checks and balances and arrive at a pleasant mixture of both philosophies.

We may find that the ideal setup is for a mom to be paired with a dad as head coach and assistant coach. That way, we might be assured that our kids will receive the full measure of benefits that sports can confer, while preventing any single coaching style from predominating.

41.

Don't Try to Be a Crowd Pleaser

EVERYONE LOVES APPROVAL. If you're coaching, it's only natural to want your players to like you. You'll also want to get along with referees and league officials, and of course, you want to please your fellow parents, many of whom you know from other situations.

But you'll find that the old adage "You can't please all of the people all of the time" definitely applies to coaching. The reason is simple: a single strategic decision will have an impact on nearly everybody present—including the people who are sitting in the stands.

For example, let's say you're losing a baseball game by a lopsided score. The opposing pitcher is doing very well, but you can detect the signs of fatigue. Most observers would love it if one of your players could rattle the pitcher by blasting a double, a triple, or—if Providence would have it—a home run.

But you decide that, being behind by five runs or more, you really need base runners. So, you start using the take sign, which requires your hitters to allow pitches to go by without swinging.

To some parents, this appears to be a "wimpy" strategy. In fact, when I was discussing this book with an editorial assistant, she said that she thought taking pitches was "cheating" on the part of the manager!

In any case, her feelings aren't all that unusual. Parents will want their kids to be visible heroes, and you don't become one by letting balls go by—even if it gets you on base and scores runs for your team.

But it is an absolutely sound strategy if you want to get back into the game and have a chance of prevailing. Only a few of your parents will readily appreciate this fact.

A similar strategic situation can arise when you need to advance a base runner to scoring position. You might ask one of your better hitters who steps to the plate to bunt.

Bunt? Am I kidding? This is what parents could be wondering. They want fireworks, and I mean the big stuff. Bunting is hardly a sparkler, by comparison. Where's the thrill in that?

Of course, you probably know what I'm leading up to. **If you succumb to the pressures of the crowd to entertain them with huge sports moments, you and your team will suffer.**

Taking pitches and bunting are essential parts of the game of baseball. Major leaguers do these things because they work. Moreover, they're really important when you're coaching young people, because both activities train young batting eyes and create disciplined individuals who are able to put the greater good before their own interests in achieving glory.

There is a good reason, other than safety, that there is a fence between the bleachers and the playing field. It is to separate you and your players from the undue influence of observers.

Do everyone a favor: ignore the crowd and try to please yourself instead.

42.
Handling the "Loudmouthed" Parent

Go to nearly any professional sporting event, and you're bound to hear one person's voice bellowing over everyone else's. Like a newborn, this individual will have an uncanny capacity to yell, hour after hour, without experiencing any audible signs of fatigue.

Nearly everyone around will be cringing. You'll pray that this person will go for a hot dog and never return. Unless he or she has season seats next to yours, you'll have to put up with it for only one game.

But the presence of a loudmouthed parent when you're coaching can be a curse for an entire season.

Not only are such people a distraction for other parents and fans, but more important, they'll also tend to confuse and upset your team. For instance, they'll bark out untimely commands to hitters—like "Swing away!" or "Don't just stand there!"—after you have explicitly given the player a take sign.

Caught in the middle of these competing instructions, kids will freeze up, not wanting to make a mistake. Then, they'll blame themselves for failing to perform.

How can you lower the decibel level of a loudmouth? Do it indirectly, through the instrumentality of other parents. Ask them if they feel their kids are being distracted by the offender's excessive vocalizations.

They'll probably say, "Oh, him! Yeah, he is loud, isn't he? Well, I'm sure he could have an impact on the kids." By merely planting this seed, you'll set into motion the wonderfully subtle process of invoking group control over the miscreant.

Parents will start to sanction him, largely through nonverbal behavior. When he yells out, they'll frown at him instead of ignoring him. They may sit farther away from him in the bleachers, making him feel isolated.

A few may engage him in conversation to distract him. And one or two may ask him to tone it down a little. The key is that *you* shouldn't have to micromanage what happens in the stands as well as what happens on the court or the field.

You already have your hands full, trying to bring out the best from your team while helping them to have a good time. Moreover, the last thing you need is a loudmouth who decides to wage a personal war with you and your coaching style because you have personally criticized him.

Of course, this is one more topic that you can handle in your preseason remarks to parents. You might mention how sensitive kids are, and how they can misconstrue innocent remarks as being hostile critiques, especially if they're communicated in a loud voice.

Once I heard a parent yell out to a girl who tried to steal second base, "You, of all people, shouldn't be stealing!" He was referring to the fact that she was overweight, so it was an especially cruel remark. It was also blatantly wrong.

I want all of my players to steal bases, and this player happened to be reasonably quick on her feet, plus she was a real competitor. She *wanted* to be fast on the bases, and that's more than half the battle in her league.

After hearing the loudmouth's misplaced critique, I chatted with her when she reached third base. Looking her in the eye, I told her, "You're *good* on the bases, and you're going to be one of our *best* base stealers."

And that's exactly what she became, to the delight of everyone, and to the chagrin of one particular loudmouth.

43.

Handling the Challenger

ABOUT 75 PERCENT of all the parents you'll meet will happily stay in the background. They may or may not come to your games, but if they do, they'll be content to merely cheer for their kids, if they cheer at all.

Otherwise, you wouldn't know they're there. But you'll encounter one person, generally a dad, who will definitely make his presence known. I refer to him as the Challenger.

Perhaps in his day, he was a pretty good player, so he tends to show off. He could be a big fan of the pro leagues and feel that he knows a thing or two about the game.

Challengers won't be very happy with your coaching strategies, and they'll let you and everyone else know it—usually in the most vocal manner. But because they have a right to cheer, they'll cloak their criticisms through that medium.

For instance, if you're the type of coach who de-emphasizes the importance of winning, they'll challenge this premise.

They'll grumble from the stands, "Why aren't you giving them the take sign? Their pitchers can't even reach the plate!"

"Well," you'll think, "I do use the take sign, but I also like to give my players a chance to swing at the ball. And this game is more fun for them if they learn to *hit*."

Then, you'll catch yourself: "Why am I even dignifying that remark of his?" In that instant of self-perception, you'll appreciate that challengers make you second-guess your decisions. They seize your concentration, and by doing so, they pull your head out of the game.

The very same guy who will challenge you for not putting on the take sign, could rap you for having your kids swing away. In other words, there's no pleasing him.

How come? Because he secretly covets your job. He wants to coach, but he doesn't have the time, patience, or courage to formally volunteer.

My view is that it's better to have a potential challenger inside the tent than outside. So, give him something to do. Ask him to bring his glove to practice. (I'll bet you even money that he has one, and it's calling out to him in his dreams!) If he doesn't have one, lend him one of yours. Have him warm up your pitcher, or play catch with anyone, for that matter.

While he does this, you should do something else. This not only will make him feel important, which is nice for him, but also will give you an extra helper, which you can always use.

Plus, it will open a direct communication channel from him to you—a private channel. The next time he has the bright idea of putting the take sign on, he'll be more inclined to whisper it to you through the chain-link fence instead of broadcasting it from the stands.

Who knows, like a broken clock, a challenger can even be "right" about something once or twice a day. Remember: It doesn't hurt to hear another point of view every now and then—providing it's intended to help and not simply to disparage your coaching capabilities.

44.

The Political Parent

PARENTS COME IN all sizes, shapes, and dispositions.

Some will be pillars of the community. Others will be on parole for assault and battery. And by looking at them, you won't consistently be able to distinguish them from each other. Don't make the mistake of assuming that everyone automatically adheres to a code of civility and politeness simply because their children are involved in the activity you're coaching.

Sooner or later, you'll interact with the "backstage politician." This person may have had experience with parental politics in other situations. Because backstage politicians have some organizational experience, they know how institutions think and behave.

If you get on their wrong side, they can hurt you and, by doing so, hurt the team. Their venom will be aimed at you, but their wrath won't really be "about" you.

It will be about *power*. Politicos enjoy wielding it. They need an adversary or a hot issue to keep their talons sharp. So, if you make any "transgression," such as changing the offspring's playing position or sanctioning the kid for being late, you'll come under fire.

It won't be direct fire. It will be more like guerrilla warfare. You won't necessarily see the enemy; you'll only feel his or her destructiveness.

For instance, such types may start a whispering campaign to get back at you. They could ask other parents in the stands "Why's *he* coaching— do you know?" There is no suitable answer to this question. It attacks motivations, competence, and performance at the same time.

Or, they may ask their peers "Do you *like* his coaching style?" This can put people on notice that you may be a poor fit for the post. If subtle means don't work, they'll possibly hang a moniker on you like "the Coach from Hell."

At some point, one parent will come to you to report that other, unnamed parents aren't too happy with what you're doing. The messenger won't divulge names and will be vague about what you need to remedy, which happens to be out of whack.

Next, a league representative may casually mention to you that parents are grumbling. What started as a molehill will suddenly look like Mount Everest. You'll be facing what seems to be a granite wall of opposition.

What can you do if you're caught in this situation? There are a few moves you can make:

• You can ask for a formal meeting with your accuser and the league. This way, you can refute any "charges" against you. If they're spurious, they'll dissipate, and it's unlikely they'll recur.

Of course, the downside to doing this is you invest the league with the formal authority to manage the conflict. If the board is filled with spineless protoplasms, you could find that you're slimed by the encounter, or that you've lost your ability to manage in your comfort zone, using your natural "style."

• You can smile when you hear the criticism, nod your head, and thank the people for coming forward to share their feelings. Then, you can continue coaching as if nothing had happened.

• You can personally confront the politician. I wouldn't do this, because the person is probably well versed in putting "spins" on conversations. The spin doctor will emerge as a sympathetic victim, and you'll seem like a bully. These types turn the tables to their advantage.

An alternative is to speak to the person in the presence of one of your fellow coaches. This will inhibit the expression of a certain degree of hostility and keep the encounter within bounds. It will also provide you with a witness, which will limit the parent's spin-doctoring capabilities.

Politicians can be exceedingly distracting. Nonetheless, try to focus on what counts, and that is coaching the kids—even if some of their parents try to intrude into the process.

45.

It's Wise to Ignore Certain Things

IN MY EXPERIENCES coaching, I've learned to let certain negative comments slide right off. For instance, one baseball team that I coached was having a rough three or four games. We lost them all, and not by tiny margins.

What I had worked on in practices seemed to be completely forgotten by game day. So, I decided that we were going to be unbelievably aggressive on the base paths. If we couldn't outpower or outpitch our adversaries, we'd rattle them by outrunning them.

Whenever we had a base runner, the steal sign was put on. Then, when she'd arrive at second, she'd steal third. And, yes, I'd even have her steal home.

It worked so well that we started crushing other teams. My players showed more life than I had seen all season. Every one of them was super-aggressive, and it was something truly beautiful to behold.

After one game, a parent came up to me and whispered that some of our opponents were peeved because we seemed to be "running up the score." I couldn't believe my ears. This particular parent was one of *ours*. He had witnessed the prior games, when we got trounced, but now that we were the conquerors, he was the messenger of the bad news that it wasn't good form to win big, as others had.

Instead of getting out of sorts over his comment, I privately laughed myself silly. This critique was absurd. I realized, really for the first time, that there was no such thing as "winning" if you were the coach. You can't win if you seek endorsements of other people—especially parents.

Moreover, I started to embrace a theory I had heard from time to time: you have to play your own game, and not anyone else's.

Coaching is one of the few human activities that resists collaboration. You're going to be the loser if you allow your style to be informed by the perceptions of those on the sidelines.

I don't mean that you can't ask for somebody's opinion from time to time. I'm saying that your confidants should be either other coaches on your team or complete outsiders who have no vested interest in your team or your league. This way, you'll be able to hear their feedback, evaluate it, and carry on without feeling that you must implement it.

Trust your instincts. Be yourself. Don't look over your shoulder. And learn to ignore certain things.

PART VI

Referees, Umpires, and League Officials

46.

Umpires and Referees: The Incompetent

I'M A FIRM believer that if you fight with an umpire, you're bound to lose.

Generally, they're not going to change a call, even if they were blatantly wrong and everyone knows it. Pushing them just doesn't work, and it can easily backfire.

At the same time, you need to put referees and umpires on notice that you're aware of their miscues and that they need to pay closer attention to what's going on. No umpire wants to get complained about to league officials, and be sanctioned.

Like most of us, umpires report to somebody, and they can be called on the carpet if they're utterly incompetent. But this is small consolation if you're losing by a basket at the buzzer, and they ignore a blatant foul against your shooter.

What you can hope for is that they'll silently recognize their error, and then redeem themselves by giving your team the benefit of the doubt in a later play or the next contest that they officiate. It has been my experience that if you treat the most reckless of refs with a degree of respect, you'll be rewarded.

It has happened to me on several occasions. An umpire will blow a call, and one of my assistant coaches will start to blow up. I'll jump up to prevent my associate from being ejected, and the game will continue.

Then, out of nowhere, we'll be handed a favor. One of our players who should be called out for throwing her bat about twenty feet will reach base safely. The ump will simply stare at me and nod his head but remain silent.

I'll nod back, while donning a serious look to signify that I realize my player got a free pass on that play. I'll be expected to correct her right away, which I'll do if she is standing on a base that I'm coaching. If I'm near our dugout, I'll gravely remind my players that they shouldn't throw their bats.

This entire sequence is like a ten-second morality play. We erred, we were forgiven, and we showed proper contrition. So, before you write off your official as hopeless, remember that even the worst sinner may find a way to be redeemed.

47.

Umpires and Referees: Beware of the Executioner

SOME UMPIRES AND refs are known to be tough. They relish situations in which they have to make difficult calls. Half of the fun for them seems to be in intimidating players, coaches, parents, and anyone who dares to get into their crosshairs.

When they call balls and strikes or fouls and penalties, they don't make simple announcements: they shriek out their judgments. It's not just a call that they're making. It's a sentence imposed by a hanging judge.

Let's say a pitcher throws a ball. Executioners won't be satisfied to shake their heads and say in a barely audible voice, "Ball one." They'll yell, "Nooooo! Ball *one!*" It's like a personal rebuke to the pitcher.

And this is the problem with executioners. They make their judgments sound as if they *are* aimed at players. As you can imagine, this creates a defensive atmosphere. I've seen kids tremble and cower in their presence.

When I was growing up, there was an executioner in our Little League. By day, he was a history and physical education teacher at my school. He was known as a disciplinarian, and kids were crazy to cross him.

One day, he ordered me to serve a term of detention, for some minor playground infraction. I arrived superearly and persuaded the detention monitor to let me go slightly before the end of my sentence. I was a starter on our school's basketball team, and detention was going to conflict with an important game against our city rival at the local high school.

The second I got out, I rode my bike as fast as I could to the game. It was about two miles away. I arrived at halftime, and my coach immediately inserted me into the contest as play resumed. It was a tough battle, and by the end, we were lucky to walk away with a tie.

Guess who the referee was at the game? It was none other than our local executioner. After the contest, he raced up to me and barked, "When I give you detention, you're supposed to go!"

"I did!" I defended.

"Then, you left early!" he responded.

"I got there early, and I put in the time, and then I was excused, and I came here," I breathlessly explained.

"The next time you get detention, you're *ineligible*, understand?" he admonished.

"OK," I said, summoning my best look of contrition. I was deeply concerned that sooner or later, he'd find a way of paying me back.

If your team ever faces an executioner, warn your players to avoid arousing the tyrant's wrath.

Luckily, I never had to face that particular problem again. I graduated within a few months of our spat. Though the years roll by, I'll never forget the game that I almost missed. The executioner kept me out of the first half, which hurt my team. But we definitely rallied in the second half, and the baskets I sank helped a lot.

It was one time that a tie felt like a personal victory. And a welcomed reprieve!

48.

What Can You Do About the Blatantly Biased Referee?

UMPIRES AND REFEREES are human, which means they're as corruptible as anyone else.

They may have a special interest in seeing one team win or another team lose. A given referee might be best pals with a mom or dad who is sitting in the bleachers, or may feel that he or she was shown disrespect by a team's manager during a prior game, and it's time for some old-fashioned payback.

The ref could even have a relative who is playing on one of the teams. This has happened to me. I was coaching a game in which one of my players was closely related to the ref. She told me this at the beginning of the game, and I found it disconcerting.

You might be thinking, who am I to complain if she's on my team and the ref wants to see his relation do well and win? But it bothered me for several reasons:

1. It couldn't help but introduce bias into the game. Even if he bent over backward to avoid doing us any favors, that alone would taint his judgment.

2. How could I coach her objectively and fairly if I felt my judgment was being second-guessed by the ref? Could I take her out of the game if I needed to insert another player, or would I have to keep her in so I could appease his interest in seeing her play?

3. What if he gave our team more of the close calls, and they made the difference in determining the final score? How would I feel about that? What if I were an opposing coach and discovered later that the ref had been biased?

Leagues should require referees to disclose any obvious conflicts they would have in officiating games. A clear question to ask is if they have any relatives who are active players on teams with which they will be coming into contact.

If so, they could be excused from officiating in those games, in the same way that judges recuse themselves from presiding over cases in which they have a special interest or professional conflict.

Umpires and referees will never be totally free from bias, but their fundamental duty is to rise above it. We should remove temptation by helping them to avoid obvious conflicts before they arise.

49.
League Officials: The Straddler

DURING MY FIRST year as a Little League manager, I experienced problems with some parents who had committed their children to so many extracurricular activities that the kids were chronically absent from my team's practices and games.

That year, we had fourteen kids on our roster, and we had to get each kid into every game, for at least a few innings. So, those who didn't want to make an effort to attend were a special burden when they did show up.

I wanted to find out what the procedures were in our league for dropping kids from the roster. So, I contacted an official, and I couldn't quite believe what I heard:

"Actually, there are no rules that are in place for dropping players," the official said.

"What does that mean?" I asked.

"Well, you have to come before the board, present the facts, and then we'll make a decision on a case-by-case basis."

In other words, judgments were made in an ad hoc manner. As a manager, I could establish a team rule, have it be broken by a player, but then find that the league wouldn't necessarily support my decision.

When I expressed my dismay over this situation, another official explained that by not having standards and rules, they could be as flexible as they needed to be in any situation.

There is a word for this posture. It's called "straddling." Officials who straddle will always find themselves in the middle of disputes because they want to retain most of the power for themselves. This denies coaches the ability to predict whether their decisions will be backed up when the chips are down.

If you're dealing with straddlers, don't act first and explain later. Do it the other way around. Devise your own team rules, and get the board to agree in advance that they're reasonable.

When you encounter a rule breaker, advise the parent that you're going to act unless the offending behavior is changed. Then, inform the league.

Only after doing so should you act. By following this procedure, you'll discourage potential straddlers from frustrating your efforts or reversing your decisions.

50.
Beware of the Negligent League Official

THE CHARGE OF negligence can rightly be made when somebody who has a duty to exercise a degree of care in dealing with others falls short of that standard. The baby-sitter who pays more attention to her boyfriend than to her client is acting negligently. League officials throughout kids sports can act negligently as well.

Here are some typical scenarios of which you should be aware so that you can take action if necessary:

• Officials might fail to provide teams with safety kits, a sufficient number of helmets, or other protective devices. They might try to support their inaction by citing budgetary cutbacks or lack of sponsors, but these are excuses that shouldn't be accepted.

If your team doesn't have the right equipment to assure the safety of players, be loud enough and persistent enough to get what you need. If necessary, I'd consider purchasing these items myself and then billing the league. If they refuse to reimburse the cost, you can threaten to take them to small-claims court to seek recovery.

• League officials are negligent if they fail to provide playing fields or courts with sufficient lighting, forcing teams to play in dangerous degrees of darkness. When I was playing in Pony League, a friend of mine was struck in the face by a fly ball that he couldn't track because of the poor lighting conditions. He had to undergo plastic surgery.

Likewise, if officials insist that games be played on unsuitable surfaces, such as rain-soaked fields, they could be liable for the injuries sustained because of their failure to close the fields or to disallow play until the unsafe conditions abate.

• League officials may be negligent if they know that there is dangerous gang activity in the parking lots adjacent to fields, before, during, or after games, and they fail to notify police or take corrective action. This could include hiring security officers to patrol the areas.

I envision a time when security personnel will be hired as a matter of course by leagues, not only to diminish the danger from criminals but also to reduce threats of bodily harm from enraged players, coaches, parents, and umpires.

• Speaking of violence, if a league official has reason to believe that a given player, parent, coach, or umpire/referee poses an imminent danger, yet does nothing to warn the person or people who are threatened or to protect them, I believe the official could be found legally negligent.

• If league officials fail to provide coaches with sufficient training to be effective in their roles, then I believe they also are negligent. A formal training program should be made available to all new coaches in all organized sports leagues. It is available in the YMCA's Y-Winners program, mentioned elsewhere in this book. The training is quite helpful.

If you feel that your league officials' conduct or failure to act in a timely or appropriate way is threatening the well-being of anyone associated with the sport, bring it to their attention. Take other corrective measures if you must. Remember, many of the folks who serve as league officials may be exceedingly nice, but this doesn't mean they're necessarily competent as well.

PART VII

TIPS FOR CONDUCTING PRACTICES AND GAMES

51.

"Does Everybody Have a Parent Here, or a Ride?"

ONE SUMMER, MY wife and I took our daughter to Monterey for a vacation. By chance, we discovered a place with a playground that is just short of heaven—if you're a small-fry. It's "Dennis the Menace Park," and it's filled with neat things kids can climb, like a big, black locomotive.

Our daughter was so swept up in the atmosphere that before we could stop her, she vanished. Instantly, my wife and I split up to find her. After five nerve-racking minutes, we finally saw her running around, hand-in-hand with another child.

I can't tell you how awful it felt to allow her to slip beyond our immediate supervision. I vowed to never let that happen again, and fortunately, it hasn't.

I suppose that experience made me somewhat of a stickler when it comes to supervising the kids we coach. During water breaks, if they have to walk anywhere out of sight to reach a drinking fountain, one of the coaches or a parent will accompany them. They'll also be guided to bathrooms.

I always try to end practices at the same time, so parents know exactly when to pick up their kids. Before concluding, I always ask, "Does everyone have a parent here, or a ride home?"

If I hear a single "no," or if I detect that a shy kid doesn't want to admit that his or her parent is late, I'll double-check: "Are you *sure* you have a ride?" More times than not, the quiet child needs a lift.

As the coach, you should arrange with parents in advance what to do in case a ride doesn't show up. You have three options: (1) You can wait with the players whose parents are running late; (2) You can drive these kids home; or (3) You can arrange to have another parent or coach take them home.

None of these options is ideal. It would be great if all parents showed up on time, but that's not going to happen. My choice has usually been to stay late, waiting with the rideless kids. After twenty or thirty minutes elapse, I'll then drive them home.

It's handy to have a phone with you so players can call their folks to see if they're delayed for a particular reason. It would be wise to give this number to parents, so they can call you at the end of events to notify you that they're stuck or running late.

Under no circumstances are kids to be left by themselves to wait for errant chauffeurs. I don't care if there are three or four kids who seem capable of keeping each other company. Sooner or later, one of them will be left alone and will become vulnerable to any number of dangers.

52.

How Hard Should You "Push" the Kids?

ANNIE HAS A lot of potential as an athlete. Maybe she won't be a pole-vaulter or a high jumper or a basketball player. But nature seems to have endowed her with a perfect "catcher's body." She has a stout, rugged exterior, and for a ten-year-old, she has some good baseball instincts.

But she seems lazy. Her dad isn't much help because he's habitually nonpunctual. She frequently misses practices, and instead of arriving at a game forty-five minutes early, as everyone is asked to do, she's lucky to arrive five minutes before the umpire yells, "Play ball!"

You, on the other hand, are a competitor. This is one of the reasons you decided to coach in the first place. You want to field a team that has a chance of winning the championship, not only this year, but next year as well. To do this, you need to have a capable catcher. At the rate she's going, Annie is probably going to regress instead of progressing.

What should you do? Should you aggressively coach her and try to develop her to her highest potential, despite the flakiness of her parent? Or, should you just shrug your shoulders and let her rise or fall to whatever level she finds herself in the normal course of events?

In other words, how hard should you push her to develop her talents?

As with so many other issues in coaching, this one gets back to values. One of my goals at the beginning of any sports season is to improve the skills of my players. Generally, I announce this in my "speech to the troops" when we assemble for our first practice.

The improvement we're here to achieve is more than being better at playing the sport when the season ends. A certain amount of growth is inevitable, providing they're dedicated and they play hard. Discounting this taken-for-granted progress, I judge my success by asking myself, Have I left them better than I found them with respect to their abilities?

Can they do things that they couldn't do before, such as make solid contact with pitches that they used to miss by a mile?

If you wish to produce substantial improvement, you'll need to communicate challenging expectations. In words and in deeds, you need to get across the point that it's normal for players to stretch in their abilities, and that they should expect to outdo the "personal bests" that they've achieved in the past.

This means that you're going to push them—to some extent.

In the case of Annie and her dad, if you comment that she has some natural gifts, you're going to immediately put into motion higher expectations for her performance. Implicitly, you'll be saying that there's a gap between how good she is and how good she can be.

This is a compliment, but it's also a challenging message. It disturbs complacency. It says that achieving at current levels isn't good enough; it's beneath her.

Three things can happen if you bring this observation to their attention:

1. If they don't want to improve, they might resent the comment and become even more detached. Their response could be translated: "Leave us alone!"

2. They may not believe the message, or even if they do, they may feel that she's sufficiently talented as it is, so she doesn't have to try any harder.

3. They may appreciate that you are trying to bring out her best and that you have taken special notice of her potential.

Whenever we make a correction or offer a helpful tip, we're saying, "You can do this better. You can be a better player." Be aware that some parents will resent the special attention you're willing to provide. They'll interpret it as undue pressure.

Annie's parent actually told me, "I know you think she has potential, but I don't want her corrected. I'll do that—it's my job as a parent."

After hearing that, I reluctantly backed off and allowed nature to take its course.

53.

How Frequent Should Your Practices Be?

HOW OFTEN SHOULD you schedule practices?

This is a basic question upon which there isn't 100 percent agreement. Let's examine some of the issues involved:

• Your practice schedule may be a result of following a tradition that a previous coach set for the team. If you have a slew of returning players and parents, there's usually some merit in sticking to the status quo.

For one thing, you won't violate their expectations. That's definitely a plus. For another, the prior coach's practice schedule may be adequate to accomplish the task of preparing your players.

• The frequency of your practices will also be determined by the calendar. Are you still in preseason? If so, you may want to schedule two practices per week to get your team into shape.

When the actual playing season gets underway and you're playing a game or two a week, I'd cut back to one practice per week, so you won't exhaust the players. You should still require players to arrive at the field or court at least a half hour to an hour before each game for loosening up and drilling.

• I'm not here to exhaust my players, or place undue demands on their parents. Therefore, I believe less is more when it comes to the number of practices I schedule. However, you also have to consider that unless you make your sport demanding enough, physically and mentally, your players could lose interest. They need reasonably frequent opportunities to be reinforced—to perceive, by playing and practicing, that their skills are improving.

• A certain critical mass is also reached with respect to developing a sense of common mission and "teamness" when you get together at least three times a week, whether for the purpose of practicing or for playing games. Friendships develop through frequency of contact: the more we see of certain people, the more probable it is that we'll bond with them.

So, if you had all the time in the world to coach your team, how much of it would you be wise to allocate for the purpose of practicing? If you're like me, you'll probably find that two to three times per week is fine for the preseason, dropping back to one or two times per week once games begin.

There is one exception: holidays. How many practices should you schedule during holiday weeks? If you're facing Christmas break and your soccer season extends into January and beyond, I suggest you poll your players and parents to see how many will be in town and available to attend practice. (Assuming you and your co-coaches won't be gone.)

You'll likely find that some kids will be available the first part of the holiday period, and others will be available the latter part. So, you may want to schedule some practices for these "bookend" periods. Even if only half or fewer of your players make it to a holiday workout, I think you'll find that the kids are grateful for a chance to socialize and to have some structured recreation during these times.

54.
Helping Kids to Overcome Their Fear of Injury

ONE OF THE most exciting plays in baseball occurs when a runner is rounding third base and speeding toward home plate just as the ball arrives. The catcher sweeps a tag onto the foot of the runner, and in a cloud of dust, the umpire calls the runner "Out!" or "Safe!"

Sliding and tags are so commonplace in professional baseball, as well as in high school and senior municipal-league play, that we forget how *scary* these behaviors are to new players. If you're nine, and you've never had to slide before, it can seem complicated.

We're telling kids to run and, as they're running, to kick up their legs and to scrape along the ground on their bottoms. While all this is happening, they're supposed to maintain their forward momentum, not slow down as their foot plows into the bag.

They have to wonder what will happen if their legs get twisted like pretzels. And won't they tear their pants and cut and bruise their knees? And even if these things don't occur, how will they handle the embarrassment and injury to their egos if they look like flailing guppies?

Here's how I teach sliding:

1. I explain its purpose and why it's absolutely necessary to the game of baseball or softball. (You'd be amazed at the number of kids who think they can have superb careers in these sports without ever having to slide! We have to tell them that sliding is inevitable.)

2. I show them how it's supposed to be done. I get down on the ground and demonstrate exactly what the legs should be doing. For fun—and I don't expect the neophytes to get this down pat— I demonstrate both "straight" slides as well as "hook" slides.

3. I ask for volunteers who are veterans at sliding. They do a few, and then the novices start warming up to the idea.

4. Then, I ask for volunteers among those who haven't done it before. You can expect one or two of the youngest to be bold enough to try.

5. Finally, I ask everyone to line up at first base to take turns running into second and sliding.

A few will refuse to risk it, or else they'll take off for second and think better of the idea before they reach the bag. That's OK. I'll say, "Good try—you'll catch on."

And they will. They'll see their teammates enjoying it and doing it without injury. This can go far in persuading reluctant kids to keep trying. Before long, they'll slide safely in an actual game and be thrilled with their accomplishment.

When that happens, they will have conquered their fear of injury.

55.

How to Teach Sports Theory

ONE EVENING, I was discussing baseball coaching strategies with my wife, who is quite involved with our teams. I started to tell her about the thoughts that should course through a player's mind as a baseball game unfolds:

"If I'm playing center field, and I notice that the hitter has fouled off a fastball to the right side, I'll move to my left because he's swinging late. That is, I'll move if I can read the catcher's sign and I see that another fastball is coming. If it's a change-up or a slider, I may hold my ground because a late-swinging hitter may send that right up the middle.

"If I've had no experience with that hitter at all—say he's from out of town, I'll do what I did as a catcher. I'll watch how he strides to the plate, where he plants his feet, and how he takes his practice swings. That plus his body type will help me to guess how he's going to swing."

This bit of analysis flew out of my mouth so fast, and so casually, that my wife was blown away.

"You actually go through all of those mental steps?" she asked, incredulous.

"Sure, and then, on every pitch the situation changes, and you have to know how many outs there are and how many runners are on base, and predict what they're going to do and rehearse what you'll do if the ball is hit to you, on a fly, or on the ground—and whether it's hit softly or hard—you know . . ."

"How can you ask *kids* to be thinking about all of that stuff?" she challenged.

My answer to her was, "You need to teach them sports theory, even if they don't understand it all right away."

Teaching sports theory is essential to helping people of all ages to enjoy sports—whether they're players or spectators. The more they know, the more they'll be able to appreciate.

A person who actively uses his or her head in a game can have inferior physical skills yet still achieve at above-average levels. A player who has both physical and mental capabilities can become a champion.

I've found that the easiest way to teach theory is by building on the innate tendency of kids to construct theories of their own. They're always wondering why things happen the way they do, so why not start by asking them what they're already picking up on.

If we have been outplayed by another team, I like to ask: "Why do you think they did so well?"

It's open-ended, and it gently leads to a discussion of their strengths as well as our shortcomings. Believe it or not, even first-graders are powerful theory-builders. One of my third-grade basketball players responded to my query with this pithy observation: "They passed the ball to each other."

I can't tell you how much it was worth to the team for her to have made that observation on her own. She was right, of course. The other team really played as a team, and passing was a big part of their winning style.

By comparison, no matter how much I would cajole and coax, I couldn't get my players to pass often enough. They'd keep the ball to themselves and either take wildly improbable shots or simply wait to be stripped of the ball.

After our player's acute observation, passing became a big part of our game as well. Do you know why her comment made such an impact?

It came from her lips, so she and her teammates owned the idea. And recognizing a sound theory when they heard one, they immediately put it to work.

56.

The Delicate Art of Assigning Kids to the "Best" Positions

As a coach, you'll quickly learn that every kid has a favorite playing position and wants to be assigned to it.

The best positions seem to be the ones that involve the most heroics. They're the ones that make the crowd cheer. They're often the "busiest" positions as well.

In baseball, pitching certainly qualifies. First base is also desirable because most infield plays involve a throw to first. Catching can be attractive, but that involves *very* hard work, a lot of sweating, and a number of bruises, so fewer young folks are attracted to it.

All three of these position players *touch* the ball a lot. They're involved in numerous plays, and this makes them feel important. It also helps them to fight boredom. If any of these position players is weak, the team will almost certainly fail to perform well.

But, there are *nine* positions in baseball, not three. How are the other players going to feel if they're not given the chance to pitch, to catch, or to play first base?

Sadly, many will feel they've been relegated to lower status unless, as coaches, we fight this tendency. Fortunately, there are several things we can do:

• Conduct tryouts for all positions at the beginning of each season. Invite any player to try any position in practice. See how they do. You may be surprised by the hidden talents that emerge. By the same token, those without talent at certain positions will be likely to see that fact for themselves, and therefore they'll clamor less for future chances at these spots.

• Develop backup players for every position. Don't let any individual "own" first base, as if it is exclusive property—no matter how good the player is at the position. You never know when an injury, or a compelling birthday party invitation, will prevent him or her from being in the lineup.

Periodically, switch personnel around. Bring in your second-string players in the later innings of games, especially when you're wildly ahead or hopelessly behind. That way, they'll gain experience in low-pressure situations.

• Avoid stereotyping. Just because Megan is tall, this does not mean that she absolutely must play first base. One of the best kids I've ever seen at that position was a coach's daughter who happened to be the smallest member of her team. (He placed the tallest at shortstop!)

• Sell your players on the importance of every position. Tell your right fielder that Raul Mondesi and Gary Sheffield fought the management of the Dodgers for the chance to play that position! Mention that the great Ken Griffey Jr. plays center field. Exclaim with awe that people who play third base have to have the quickest reflexes in the infield.

Ultimately, your job is to balance a child's genuine interest in playing a given position with his or her abilities relative to those of other players. For kids with poor ball-handling skills, a spot in the infield is probably out of the question—at least, until they show improvement.

While waiting for that to happen, we can do everything possible to make every player feel that he or she has an important, if not perfect, role to play on the team.

57.

Why Kids Love the
Wrong Drills

SHOW ME A kid who likes to do what is "good for you," instead of what's fun, and I'll show you an exceptional kid.

This can be seen in sports drills. If you ask a bunch of basketball players what they would like to do in practices, invariably they'll beam back, "Shooting!" or "Let's scrimmage!" These are terific activities, but they need to come after we have worked on other fundamentals.

If we're speaking about hoops, before kids shoot them, they should warm up. This should involve s-l-o-w s-t-r-e-t-c-h-i-n-g of the major muscle groups, followed by passing drills, and then some dribbling and sprints.

Specific plays should also be drilled so that they become second nature. The same principles apply to baseball, soccer, and every other team sport. Always, and I mean always, try to do first things first.

Can you name the favorite activity of kids when they're at baseball practice? It's batting. Everybody loves to bat. Even kids who never make contact with the ball love batting practice. But as coaches, we'd be fools to start our practices with this activity.

It takes a long time to complete, and kids can easily get bored because only one batter is "up" at a given time. Apart from the pitcher and catcher, everyone else feels passive until the ball is hit to someone.

You don't want the beginning of practice to drag—you want everyone to get instantly involved, moving his or her body. So, in baseball, start with simple warm-ups, such as by pairing up the kids to toss the ball around. Use batting as a reward later in the day.

There is another, possibly more significant reason that kids love to practice the wrong drills: they're easier to do than the right ones. The right drills feel awkward at first, if only because they force kids out of their comfort zones.

If you're coaching Little League softball or hardball, you'll find that sliding can be a scary activity for beginners. They're thinking, "Gee, if I hit really well, I may not *have* to slide!"

How are they going to learn to slide if they don't practice it? It won't spontaneously happen under game conditions if it hasn't been drilled. As with everything else that is new, learning its purposes as well as its mechanics takes a significant amount of time.

Bunting is another unpopular activity for baseball's beginners. It looks so puny—just dribbling the ball a few feet. Compared with hearing the crack of the bat as you slug a line drive, bunting is a bore.

Maybe so, but it improves a huge number of skills. Here are just three of them:

1. It gets kids to *really* watch the ball hit the bat. They won't do this when they're swinging away; instead, they'll lift their eyes above the ball as they swing.

2. It improves their timing. Placing the bat on the ball requires that we move in synch with the pitch. Bunting slows the process down so that timing becomes more subject to the batter's control.

3. It encourages hitters to track the trajectory of pitches until the last second. This makes them better spotters of off-speed pitches such as change-ups.

All of these skills translate directly into greater effectiveness when kids *are* swinging away. But if you want to teach bunting, you'd better place it before swinging away in the order of batting practice activities, or you won't get kids to drill successfully.

Whatever you do, make sure to get your less popular drills done and out of the way before you get into the "fun ones." If you don't, it'll be like encouraging your kids to eat dessert first.

58.

What Practice Should "Perfect"

You may have been impressed by one of those nifty videos being advertised on television: young kids zip balls around the diamond, smoothly picking up grounders and throwing perfect strikes from the outfield into tiny receptacles.

A former major leaguer pops off about how wonderful this training tape is, and you think: "Gee, that would really help my team to get a lot sharper!"

And it might, providing they're ready to operate at a very slick level. But if your experience is similar to mine, you'll find that your practice time has to be dedicated to much more elementary mechanics.

If you practice super-basics, your players will be far from perfect, but they may become competent.

Let's take basketball as an example. What are the three most basic things all players must learn to do? They'll need to dribble, pass, and shoot.

Under actual game conditions, these functions will have to be performed while kids are moving at a fairly fast clip. This complicates matters immensely, because kids will want to practice everything with professional flair, under game conditions, right away. Heck, they see it this way on TV and on videos, don't they?

But the old adage pertains to this situation: "You have to walk before you can run." Let me add this, when it comes to coaching anyone below the age of twelve: **You have to do it standing still before you can do it walking.**

In basketball, this means conducting passing drills in which kids stand across from each other, about ten feet apart, and learn to pass back and forth without dropping the ball too often. It may sound "babyish" to you, to them, and to parents, but this is where your practices need to begin.

The same principle applies to both dribbling and shooting. Dribbling from a stationary position is an absolute prerequisite to dribbling on the move. If a kid can't make a ball go up and down without having it get away, while standing still, it's bound to run away when the kid is moving down the court.

Jump shots and even layups have to come after kids learn to shoot in place. Otherwise, they'll never refine their ability to judge proper shooting distances, and they'll score far fewer points later on.

If their form isn't "clean" when they're standing still, it will become an uncontrolled mess when they're doing it on the move. And then it will be ten times more difficult to correct their errors because they'll be obscured by too many other variables happening at the same time.

Even once they can execute standing still, don't have them dribble, pass, and shoot at full speed, or they'll fall apart. Have them go in slow motion. This will reinforce the message that they need to refine their elementary form before they can merge it into a high-speed activity.

Highly paid professional athletes as well as amateurs get together before seasons begin to practice the basics. The pros know they need to awaken their dormant muscles, and as a general rule, they are careful not to overdo their exertion. In effect, they slow down on purpose.

Practice won't make your players perfect, but the thing we can hope to perfect is elementary form. If we succeed in this pursuit, we'll optimize our results.

59.

Water Breaks, Drill Variations, and Other Changes of Pace

WHEN YOU'RE CONDUCTING practices, make sure to have a number of drills from which to choose for a particular day. You'll need them to keep the attention of your players.

Ideally, these drills will be additive—in other words, they'll build upon each other. So, in each case, you'll begin with a simple task, done slowly. Then, it will be connected to other tasks until you have a sequence, or a set play, that the kids can do.

As you might expect, the youngest kids won't be able to sustain their concentration on any single activity for more than ten or fifteen minutes at a time. For instance, if you're coaching really young kids—say first through third grade, plan on having five or six drills to get you through an hour or an hour and a half of practice.

In basketball, this means the following:

1. Have a basic dribbling drill, in which each kid dribbles in place. I wouldn't spend more than five minutes with this one.

2. Next, have them dribble to half-court. Start with their "natural" hand—right or left.

Later in the practice, you might return to this drill and have them use their weaker hand. To build the challenge, you can have each drill start in slow motion and then build up the speed.

3. Follow dribbling with a passing drill in which pairs of kids pass to each other. Have them bounce the ball once in the course of passing it to the other player. Next, have them pass the ball in the air.

4. Tie together the dribbling and passing drills. Have them dribble to half-court and then pass the ball to the next player, who will dribble back and pass it off.

5. Next, have them form two or three lines and stand about ten feet from the basket. Have them shoot, rebound the shot, and pass back to the next player in line, and so on.

6. Next, position half of your players out of bounds near a basket. The other half should be at half-court. One at a time, have a player dribble and pass to someone at half-court. Then, have the half-court player dribble, shoot, and rebound. That player then dribbles back to half-court and passes off, and the next person dribbles, shoots, and rebounds, and so on.

I wouldn't go for more than twenty minutes without having some sort of water break or change of pace to refresh the kids and increase their attention spans.

If you see them yawning or spinning off into conversation groups, instead of barking at them, change drills or take an official break. This will enable you to avoid becoming an unrelenting disciplinarian, and you'll all have a lot more fun and get a lot more accomplished.

One more thing: If you're stumped for a drill that you can do, ask your players if they have one or if they'd like to make one up. They'll enjoy this "empowerment," and you'll wind up having another drill that you can draw upon.

60.

Fun and Hard Work: Why We Need Both

WHAT WOULD YOU do if you won the lottery and you never had another financial worry? Would you ever punch a time clock again?

Imagine—you would never have to answer to anyone in order to put bread on the table. In fact, you wouldn't even have to get out of bed in the morning. You could hire people to do that for you! (Well, almost!)

Would this make you happy? Would you feel fulfilled?

A lot of people would think so, but I'm not so sure. In fact, I believe that working, in some form or other, is essential to our well-being. Even if we have the potential to never work again and could spend all of our time on the golf course, we'd inevitably turn our recreation into work. (If nothing else, we'd obsessively work on improving our game!)

Work feels good. I don't mean work that is completely imposed and regulated by others, but work that is freely chosen. It is a reliable way for a person's creative impulses to find a constructive outlet.

If you think I'm overstating the necessity of working, consider the fate of a number of retirees. After some people are forced into retirement, it isn't unusual for them to lose the desire to live. Their "gold watch" becomes a cruel reward, signifying that they have gained back all of their time but have lost a large measure of their worth, at least to the world of work.

To counteract this diminution in esteem, many throw themselves into volunteer work, or take any job, just to be busy, and to feel that they're making a difference.

I don't think we're ever too old to keep working, or too young to start. Kids benefit from mowing lawns, washing the family's car, taking out the trash, and performing other chores. They learn responsibility, cooperation, and the importance of contributing to the greater good.

In the same spirit, for sports to become truly enjoyable, kids need to work hard at them.

They need to learn rules, learn competitive strategies, learn the mechanics of their positions, and above all practice to make their movements second nature. All of these endeavors really tax an individual. They aren't automatic in the least.

The benefit is that when young athletes apply themselves in these ways, they enjoy the same sensation that adults feel when they work hard: they feel *competent* at something. This builds self-image, while providing kids with a springboard from which they can leap to other achievements.

If you doubt this connection between working hard and having fun while at play, just think about a sport in which you're a below-average performer. Is it nearly as much fun to play that sport as it is a sport in which you're good?

I'm always amused by parents who subscribe to the "no pressure" school of conducting sports activities. Naively, they believe that if we "just have fun," everything will inevitably fall into place. They don't see that it takes a lot of work to create a fun atmosphere, and to produce enjoyable results, in sports or in any activity.

One parent whom I know rather well arranged for her kid's team to be managed by "no-pressure" coaches, who stressed the value of relaxing and "simply having fun." This team lost its first ten games of the season, which put the kids, the coaches, and even the most "laid-back" of parents into a funk.

Instead of practicing basic skills so the team could be more competitive on the field, the coaches would lecture the kids on how acceptable it was to lose. To me, this is like cursing the darkness while failing to light a single match.

The notion that work is work and play is play and that they should never meet is a myth. Hard work and fun aren't just correlated; inevitably, they flow from each other. Coaches and parents should appreciate that we can't have one without the other.

61.

When Should You Bring In Outside Experts?

DURING ONE GAME, my softball players were getting killed by a team from a neighboring city. I watched their pitcher throw bullet after bullet for strikes. Not only did she have an amazing fastball, but she also had a wicked off-speed change-up that made our kids twist up like corkscrews as they swung wildly at empty air.

Even more surprising was the fact that she wasn't big or muscular, as some of the best hurlers are. She was of average to small stature, but she used 100 percent of what she did have to great advantage.

Between innings, I asked the opposing coach what his pitcher was eating for breakfast. That made him smile. He volunteered that she had been working with a pitching coach for more than a year, three or four days a month, to get to where she was.

I scanned the sidelines for someone who looked like a pitching coach but didn't see any new faces. "You mean, you've been coaching her in the off-season?" I asked.

"No, she works with this pro in North Hollywood. He's one of the best. If you want to win ball games, you're going to need at least one pitcher, and hiring a coach who knows what he's doing is the way to go," he confided.

I couldn't believe it. Was I being advised to hire a professional pitching coach for nine- to twelve-year-olds? After I got over the shock, I asked how much it cost for such a service. He told me that it ranged from a hundred dollars per month on up.

"Who pays the coach?" I wondered.

"Usually, it's the kid's parent. Or a few parents get together and have the pro run some clinics. That way, it's cheaper."

This is an option that you should know about. Personally, I'm not so high on the idea. While I'm as interested in winning as the next coach, I'm not sure I'm ready to cross the divide from "amateur" to "professional" status that retaining paid, outside consultants seems to imply.

But you may be in a situation in which doing this is almost essential. For instance, let's say you've stepped up to coach a team on which the effective twelve-year-old pitchers have "graduated" to the next league. You have a young team, and nobody has been groomed by the former coach to be a pitcher.

To keep your team from getting wrecked week in and week out by teams that *do* have pitchers, you decide that you're going to have to grow some of your own—*fast*. What are your options?

You can do what I've done, which is spend some extra time of your own to cultivate the players who are interested in pitching and who seem to have the minimal skills. This can work, but even if you do a Herculean job, your new pitchers will suffer from mechanical flaws that you won't detect or be able to quickly cure. While they're still malleable, you may feel it's wiser to get outside help.

However, is it possible that you'll launch an "arms race," where competing teams will try to outspend each other to develop their respective players?

On a practical level, will you be ceding your authority as a coach to "experts" who seem to know more and thereby jeopardize your credibility and ability to lead?

Once you've hired a professional gunslinger, can your quaint Western town ever return to the peace it once knew?

You get the picture. I'm sure there are some other advantages as well as disadvantages to retaining outside experts. Feel free to pursue this option if you feel it's appropriate for your circumstances.

62.

Etiquette When Playing "Away" Games

SOONER OR LATER, one of your teams will be called upon to play on "foreign soil." This could be a high honor if you have been chosen to coach an all-star team. Or, it could be an exhibition game or a practice game before your official season has gotten under way.

In any case, you and your team will be "guests," not only on the scoreboard but also in reality. And you should act as good guests act.

Here are the top ten things you should do in order to make your visit enjoyable:

1. Brief your players on the fact that there is a heightened expectation that they'll be polite and comport themselves in a "sportsmanlike" manner. This will put them on notice that they shouldn't view this visit as a chance to goof off or to act like wise guys and gals on someone else's turf.

2. Try to arrive at the site in plenty of time to practice and to learn the contours of the court or field. You may have to create car pools if the location is off the beaten path. Otherwise, you'll find yourself in the opposite position—making excuses to delay the game while everyone is impatiently waiting for your team's members to straggle in.

3. Make a point of greeting the opposing coaches. Hand them your lineup card well in advance of the game so they don't have to ask for it.

4. Ask the opposing coaches if you can help in any way to chalk the field or prepare the scene for the game to come. While it is

usually the home team's responsibility, a helping hand might be appreciated if they're running late.

5. Smile a lot before the game begins. Allow their fans to see that you're a nice person and that it's OK for them to be friendly toward you. This has helped me out more times than I can count. By being friendly, I've been given some great pointers by opposing coaches as well as fans. They won't go out of their way for you if you seem dour or superserious.

6. Remind your players to cheer *for* their own team and not against their opponents. No razzing of any kind should be tolerated.

7. If there are hostile opposing parents, mention this to the umpires or referees, discreetly. If problems persist, alert the opposing coaches. Don't confront strangers by yourself.

8. Control your own team's parents. Remind them that they don't want any altercations, and that they have a duty to be polite and to represent the team with appropriate behavior.

9. Keep an "accountant's" eye on the scoreboard at all times, or have one of your parents sit in the scoring booth with theirs. Often, opposing scorekeepers have accidentally failed to tally the right amount of runs that we've accumulated. Once, when I pointed out that we had six runs instead of five, the scorekeeper feebly said, "Well, we've had a little trouble with lighting up the six on the scoreboard. I don't know why it does that . . ."!

10. Relax. Changing scenes could be a real refresher for you and for your players. Win or lose, it can be a lot of fun to travel to a game. So, make the most out of it.

PART VIII

Motivating Players and Recognizing Achievements

63.

A Perfect Game Can Be
Perfectly Miserable, Too

MY FIRST BIG sports loss was a hard one to swallow.

I was nine, and playing for the Rangers in a city league. The opposing pitcher was throwing smoke and had a nasty curveball.

No one could hit him, and I mean no one: He was pitching a *perfect game*. There had been no base hits, no walks, no errors. Just long faces and a growing sense of doom on the Rangers' bench.

With two down in the ninth, it was my turn to bat. I think he struck me out on three straight pitches. All I remember is that I was crushed. The game ended after my at bat. We lost 1–0.

"They beat us by scoring one lousy run! I could have made the difference if I hadn't struck out," I kept muttering. "If I had just homered, I could have tied that game. It all came down to me, and I blew it."

I was inconsolable during dinner, which my dad insisted we have at the family's favorite restaurant. The cinnamon rolls tasted bitter. The creamy Russian dressing, which I had always craved, was tasteless. My hands felt colder than the ice water.

Of course, as this mood was enveloping me, there was jubilation, I'm sure, at the pitcher's house. He had hurled a *perfect game*, for goshsakes! Was this kid on his way to the majors, or what? Why, he could write his own ticket—the sky was the limit. What an arm that kid had!

Needless to say, I survived that dark night, and I went on to have some great moments of my own in baseball. On several occasions, the game would be mine to win or lose and I'd pull through in the clutch.

The "perfect" pitcher never made it to the majors. In fact, I don't know if he ever came close to having another truly remarkable game.

I've heard professional managers say that baseball has a way of making the best of us look and feel like fools sooner or later. As coaches, we should appreciate that this is going to happen to some kid in nearly every game.

There will be the obvious "goats," who will blow the catch that could have gotten the third out to secure the victory. Less conspicuously, there will be the kid who isn't getting on base at all, when the rest of the team is cleaning up and every other player can do no wrong—or so it seems.

It doesn't take much for a kid to feel like an utter loser. We should always keep this in mind. As long as we're keeping score, it's inevitable that one team will feel dejected, and some of its members will feel the sting of defeat more acutely than the others.

Win or lose, make it a point to say to your players, "Good game!" before they leave the field or the court. That way, even if their performance wasn't perfect, they'll know you still have positive regard toward them.

Remind them that the wheel will turn. They'll have their moments of glory if they hang in there, and if they're not too hard on themselves.

64.

Should the Best Players
Play More?

WHEN I WAS in Little League, it wasn't uncommon to have one or two kids on each team who didn't really play the infield or the outfield. They didn't pitch or catch, either.

In fact, they hardly played, at all. They rode the bench most of the time because they were among the youngest on the roster and simply weren't all that good at the game. They couldn't be counted on to make the most elementary of plays. Given their limitations, hardly anyone in those days questioned the appropriateness of having them sit out countless innings.

They might see some action if their team was far ahead or far behind. Or, if it couldn't do much harm to have them come up as a pinch hitter or fill in as a pinch runner, they'd be deployed. Otherwise, they were expected to accept their ignominious fate, and the inevitable splinters that come from being bench warmers.

Today, the Little League handbook requires that all players on a team be given a minimum amount of time in each game. Generally, they must be allowed to play two innings in the field and to bat at least once.

This rule can be circumvented in certain situations—when the game is cut short because of foul weather or because one team is ahead by ten or more runs after the fourth inning—but generally, the idea is that each child has a chance to play.

Coaches can abide by this rule and still relegate some players to seeing one half of the action that others might see. For every two innings they're in, someone else may be in for four.

My question is: **Does the Little League rule go far enough?** In other words, should we strive for complete equity, where each player gets as much time in the game as the next?

For instance, in the American Youth Soccer Organization (AYSO) this year, we have twelve players on the roster. Nine can play at any given time, which means there will always be three substitutes on the sidelines.

Presuming all twelve show up for every game, it is the league's intention to give each kid the chance to play three out of four quarters in each game. Mathematically, this should produce a completely equitable result, in which no player gets more playing time than any other.

But you might wonder, where does this leave the "superstars"? You know who I mean. These are the kids who are destined for sports greatness and probable college scholarships. Do these exceptional individuals *deserve* more playing time than kids who can hardly keep up with the pace of the game?

As coaches, if we want to win, wouldn't we be fools to ever remove them from games? After all, what harm would it do to bench one of the poorest players for an extra quarter so our superstar could play all four? Heck, if our less-than-stellar players are younger, they'll probably be given more playing time later on in their sports careers, after they've had the chance to develop, right? It'll all even out sooner or later.

Sometimes it doesn't even out, though, because the player who has to sacrifice that third quarter of action so a peer can stay in the game may become discouraged and retire from organized sports before it ever becomes his or her turn to play all four quarters. Being passed over in this way might seem patently unfair to this individual.

And "fair play" is one of the traditional values that sports are supposed to uphold, right?

When I was growing up, you didn't simply sign up for Little League. You had to pass a tryout and be selected by a team. You were on notice from the very beginning that your right to play was going to be linked to your abilities. So, when the season began, if you didn't see that much action, you implicitly knew and accepted the reason, knowing also that when you improved, your time in games would increase.

Nowadays, there is a different compact between players and teams. In many leagues, there is no such thing as a traditional tryout. It is a given that a child will "make" a team and that no one will be turned away, providing the league has enough slots.

I think this come-one-come-all approach to recruiting delivers an implicit promise to kids that they won't have to compete against each other for playing time. It may be hailed by some as civilized and fair, and an idea whose time has come. But traditionalists who believe that sports are inherently competitive, and that races should go to the swiftest, could have concerns about this new direction.

This is an area in which you and your league should be clear. Whether you take the AYSO approach or one closer to the standard embraced when I was in Little League, is up to you to decide.

65.
Help Your Players to Think Positively

WHAT DO ALL of the great sports movies—*Rocky, Heaven Can Wait, The Natural,* and *Rudy,* to name just a few—have in common? They're uplifting. They portray athletes who had to overcome great obstacles to win.

Every kid you'll coach, from the weakest to the strongest, and from the least to the most talented, will come face to face with his or her limitations. When this happens, it will be your job to help them to break through and to realize their personal potential for greatness. This starts by helping them to develop a positive, can-do attitude.

For instance, during one baseball season, I coached a young player who just couldn't seem to make contact with the ball when she came to bat. She did well at the batting cage when the pressure was off, but under actual game conditions, she swung far too late.

From the third-base coaching box, I decided to try something. When she came to bat, I called out to her: "Do what you did at the batting cage. You can do it!"

I think it helped, because she blasted a line-drive base hit into center field. From that point forward, she accumulated more hits while developing the self-confidence that is wonderful to see in players.

I also coached another player who was one of our top picks in the draft. As the season began, I held high hopes for her because she seemed to have what it takes to succeed: a good throwing arm and a strong physique. But she seemed to lack even minimal self-confidence and gave up whenever any obstacle got in her way. If she bobbled a grounder, instead of shrugging it off and getting her head back into the game, she'd dwell on her error. This would spawn more miscues, and a negative cycle would ensue.

In retrospect, I think I could have done more to inspire her. I should have spent more time warming up with her before games. I should have complimented her for showing even a glimmering of the strengths that she possessed.

I believe that victories begin in our minds. If we can conceive them, we can achieve them. Planting positive visions of success is essential if you hope to bring out the best in your team. By doing this, and by teaching players to "put on their game faces" and to lift themselves into an optimistic frame of mind, you'll be giving them the gift of a lifetime.

Athletics teach people to face and to overcome adversity. This is one of the longest-lasting benefits of playing when you're a kid. Years later, when the going gets tough, you can dig back into your memory to find those critical moments when you overcame fear and hesitation, and you achieved.

That's better than money in the bank. It's the sort of can-do mentality that makes you a pleasure to work with and to be around. It puts a smile on your face and a spring into your walk because you've been a part of little miracles.

Be a relentless cheerleader for your players. Counter every negative comment you hear with a positive one. You'll be blessed by finding that while you're helping them, you'll also be helping yourself.

66.
Surviving the Humiliating Defeat

THERE IS A proven way to survive the humiliating defeat. But before I reveal it, let's define what a humiliating defeat is.

By *humiliating*, I mean the one where the score is completely lopsided. As in a 12–0 soccer or hockey shutout. Or an 84–7 football folly. Or a 25–2 softball crushing.

These aren't simple losses. They're losses of face. They make kids wonder why they can't seem to do anything right. Coaches, who thought they had thoroughly prepared their players, scratch their heads in bewilderment and start manifesting mysterious facial or bodily "tics."

You've heard about superstitious ballplayers who won't change their socks while they're on a winning streak? That's fairly eccentric behavior, right? It's nothing, zip, nada, compared with the bizarre anti-losing rituals that you'll witness after a humiliating defeat.

Coaches might begin to remove pitchers after only a few walks have been issued, or if they just feel that "she's losing her edge." Formerly aggressive managers suddenly run the game defensively. Base stealing may be discouraged, and power hitters can be reduced to bunting.

Instead of perceiving a "win" as occurring after the final whistle has been blown, teams that have been stung by humiliating defeats might start considering the "close loss"— say a score of 5–3 in baseball—as a "moral victory." You'll start hearing kids ask with a sigh, "How many more games do we have to play?"—which really means "How many more games do we have to *lose?*"

Absences become commonplace, and even the team parent, that bulwark of efficiency and cohesion, could start falling apart at the seams.

Mysteriously, parents forget that it's their turn to bring snacks, and players leave their athletic shoes at home.

Scientists have a term for this slippery slope of despair: *entropy*. Things fall apart before your eyes, like the erosion of a sandy beach after a storm.

What can we do about humiliating defeats? How can we work through the pain and keep our team together?

Here's the secret: Prepare yourself, well in advance, to humbly accept the fact that these kinds of losses will happen. This is the first and most critical step. If you entertained fantasies about having a perfect, undefeated basketball season, a big defeat could make you a basket case. But if you were slightly more modest in your aspirations, you would be able to accept a lopsided loss with a lot more tranquility.

Also, when it does happen, make sure to have a team meeting at the end of the game. Your players and parents will want to head for the hills, but don't let them scurry away.

Smile. Tell a few jokes. Laugh about it. Say "I didn't notice—did we win that game?" That'll break the tension.

Make sure you tell your players that you're proud of them.

Proud of them?

We can be proud of them for hanging in there during the game. For not quitting. For giving the best effort they could give. For acting like a team, for supporting each other. For cheering, especially when there wasn't that much to cheer about.

Tell them that the mark of champions isn't in how they act when they win, but in how well they recover from setbacks. Champions ask this question: "What can I learn from this game?"

If the opposing pitcher seemed to have been "touched by an angel" and hurled a no-hitter, the answer may be, "Not much." But if errors were made that can be remedied through better concentration and more diligent practice, then the challenges are a lot easier to address.

As a coach, you may want to sound eloquent, to strike just the right chord, but you may have to settle for this summary:

"Hey, these things happen. They played a good game, and that's nice for them. We'll get our turn to have a game like this, where we'll be in the winner's column. Let's put this one behind us and concentrate on our next game!"

67.
Appointing Captains and Team Leaders

I THINK IT's helpful to appoint team captains and cocaptains. Ideally, these are players who are advanced in age, leadership ability, and maturity. They're the kids to whom others look up and whom they naturally want to emulate.

What do these leaders do? I can't give you a "position description" because their roles are as much symbolic as strategic. But here are some of their functions:

- They often lead other players in cheering. When the emotional tide of the team needs to change, they'll be the ones who whip up the waves.

- They informally discipline your goof-offs. If Kaitlin is zoning out in the dugout, your captain might sit next to her and strike up a chat. Or, if Melody just can't keep her mind on the ball game when she's in center field, your leader will bring her attention back to planet Earth.

- They are willing to wear different hats for the good of the team. Let's say your captain is your number one scorer in soccer. It's the fourth quarter, and the other team is getting hot. You need someone who will give 100 percent at the goalie position. You can turn to your captain or cocaptain. Though they would probably have more fun scoring a goal of their own than preventing one from being scored, they're more likely to make the move without a fuss.

- They play harder, knowing that their level of play is setting an example for the rest of the group. By doing so, they'll evoke better performances from everyone.

- They reexplain your policies and directions in kid talk so teammates will understand you and your game plan.

What do they get from serving in these roles? Prestige, for one thing. I'll usually appoint one captain and two cocaptains. So, there aren't that many, which makes these roles special.

They also get a chance to be formal leaders. They shoulder responsibility and feel a greater sense of ownership of the team's results.

Do yourself a favor, though. Mention to the team that you'll be appointing your leaders after your practice season concludes and before the first game. Ask anyone who doesn't want to be considered to let you or the team parent know.

That way, you won't be stuck after appointing someone who won't give the task his or her "all." You don't want to have to demote a leader if you can avoid it.

68.

Don't "Bribe" Your Kids to Win

DURING OUR FIRST season in soccer, the head coach complimented her daughter upon scoring a goal in practice. "That's it, Judy!" she beamed. As her little one ambled toward the sidelines, she loudly whispered, "Do that during a game, and you'll get a dollar!"

I was dumbstruck. "You *pay* her to score goals?" I asked.

Sensing my incredulity, she shot back: "Sure, I do—but only a buck a goal. It's like paying them to get A's and B's in school. Everybody does that, right?"

Wrong!

I had never even considered it. But to my chagrin, I discovered that a number of parents, especially of our "high-powered" players, bribed their kids in one way or another to excel on the field.

I'm absolutely against this practice. First, it is unnecessary if your kid has the proper motivation. I believe it's entirely normal to want to do well as a player. Pride, if nothing else, propels us.

Add to this the fact that players are also trying to do something positive for their teammates, and you bring to bear enough pressure to achieve. Why a kid would need an additional, external motivation is almost incomprehensible.

Moreover, there are sound psychological reasons for avoiding money payments. The more we give, the less they'll feel they're playing for personal reasons. They'll know they're acting like mercenaries.

If you feel you have to bribe your kid to do something, double-check to see if your kid is really happy playing that sport or being on that particular team. You'll probably find that there is some problem that needs to be discussed. By adding money to the equation, you'll obscure the real issue.

If you're the coach, and it's your kid who requires the extra spiffs, it could be that you are more interested in the sport than your offspring is. That's a situation destined to backfire, and no amount of money will remedy it.

69.
Should Kids Lose Playing Time Because They've Broken Rules?

JOHNNY HAS BEEN missing a lot of practices and games. You've contacted his parents about the problem, but they just seem to make excuses on his behalf. Is it fair to give him equal playing time when you have thirteen other players who have been conscientiously coming to practices and games?

As discussed elsewhere in this section, some leagues have a rule that says every kid must be played in every game, for at least a minimum period of time. In Little League, it might mean that they have to play in the field for two innings and come to bat at least once.

The theory behind this rule is sound. What child wants to warm a bench while watching the other kids play the sport he or she signed up to play? In other words, no one signs up to watch.

But in the case of Johnny, is it fair to replace someone else to make room for him—if he has been violating team rules by not coming to practices? If the league's rule stands, then he must be played.

This removes from your coaching toolbox an important disciplinary device. If Johnny is told that he cannot play because he hasn't been practicing, it sends a powerful message to him and to his parents. It says "There are negative consequences for negative behaviors."

But I've found few leagues that are willing to discipline players or parents, or to stand behind coaches who do. Perhaps as a result of concern about negative public relations or political pressures, the unwritten rule seems to be that kids can come and go as they please, without arousing anyone's official wrath.

I think this sort of permissiveness is destructive on a number of levels. In kids' sports, we're teaching certain values that shouldn't be compromised. Here are four that are implicated in a "Johnny" type of scenario:

1. **Teamwork:** if certain kids don't feel a responsibility to be fully committed players, how can we create teamwork? Isn't a part of teamwork being there for your fellow players, to support them on the court or field?

2. **Loyalty:** if your kids are placing other activities before your practices and games, then I believe they're being disloyal to the team and to the sport.

3. **Discipline:** becoming a disciplined person is essential to achieving success in all walks of life. Honoring the clock, being on time and ready to perform, is a threshold responsibility of a maturing person.

4. **Overcoming adversity:** some kids may be absent or tardy because they feel they aren't succeeding in the sport. By facing these feelings directly, and by seeing that they can bounce back, they'll build their capacity for resilience later in life, when it counts even more.

When you agree to coach or manage a sport, review rules such as the one that requires that every kid play in every game. Quiz your league officials about whether exceptions to this rule can be made for disciplinary purposes. Run a hypothetical "Johnny" situation by them, and ask what they'd do.

You'll probably learn what discipline you can or cannot invoke. If there isn't a method for enforcing attendance or for meting out discipline, this would be a fine time to open a discussion on the subject.

70.
Awarding Game Balls
and Trophies

WHEN I FINISHED my last season as a Little Leaguer, my batting average
stood at .582. My closest rival was 150 points below that, so I was awarded
a gold medal at the annual banquet.

On the front, it showed a kid swinging a bat. On the flip side, it was
inscribed with the words "Best Hitter." As you can imagine, it meant a lot
to me because there was only one such medal that could bear those words.

That year, everyone received a trophy of some kind. If you were
elected to the all-star team, you received the standard trophy, but a star
was prominently affixed to the center of its spire. No matter what the circumstances were, receiving some symbol of participation, a statue that you
could see for years to come—well, that was, and still is, a very big deal.

Some leagues, however, don't give out trophies. That's a big mistake.

Kids treasure them. As a parent, I enjoy watching them accumulate on
my daughter's dresser. They're pretty, and they bring back fond memories.
They make everyone feel like a winner, even if you had the worst season
imaginable.

In addition to trophies, I like to award game balls to players who have
made special contributions. For example, if one of your players hits three
homers and pitches the game, the achiever deserves a small remembrance
of this special day. I'll retrieve the actual game ball and pass it around
for everyone's signature.

Of course, if the same person is the "most valuable player" game after
game, that kid would accumulate all of the balls, which could be demo-
tivating to the rest of the team. So, after a few games, this honor will
subtly shift from being bestowed based strictly on performance to include
other factors.

For instance, I might acknowledge a player who showed great courage
after being hit by a pitch. The next time she came to bat, she stood tall

in the box and then blasted a single. Her actions demonstrated to our opponents that she wasn't intimidated, while serving as an inspiration to her teammates.

Everyone on the team should be given a game ball or an equivalent badge of distinction. On the most elementary level, it's like getting a "goodie bag" at a friend's birthday party. It says, "Thanks for coming," and it wouldn't have been a party without you.

The ritual of awarding items after games also assures that coaches and managers will pay at least some attention to the positive things that occurred on the field or the court. Otherwise, especially after a loss, it would be too tempting for some to dwell on the negatives without giving the "pluses" their due.

In this spirit, I suggest you make the awarding of a game ball the *last* thing you do during a postgame meeting. Have your snacks, discuss the game briefly, and announce the following week's practice and game schedule.

Then, leave the event on a positive note. Praise the recipient, lead the applause for him or her, and then tell them you'll see them next time. That will help to sustain their positive mood until you meet again.

71.
How Wins Are Inadvertently Turned into Losses

THOUGH WINNING IS generally a whole lot more fun than losing, wins can easily lose their luster if we mishandle them. Here are some tips for being gracious in victory while assuring that our wins don't inadvertently turn into losses:

• Winning shouldn't be about beating opponents. We should really be competing against ourselves and trying to improve upon our past performances. Focusing on an outside force makes us too results oriented and less process oriented. By perfecting processes, or our athletic mechanics, we really improve.

Later in life, our kids will find that business and the professions don't improve because people are trying to beat each other. They improve because individuals and companies are trying to innovate, to draw out new things. Direct competition is more about imitation than innovation.

• Wins shouldn't be used to "prove" our superiority. They don't make us better than other players or teams in a permanent sense. They simply mean that we outscored the opposition in a given contest, or even across an entire season. That's nice, but which teams made the most progress, given the skills with which they started? Theoretically, the team that finishes dead last could be the one with more players who made more dramatic improvement than any other team—including the official champions.

• Wins don't signify that we don't need to improve. There is always room for improvement. If you don't believe this, after rising to the top in your league, just wait until you get to the play-offs or to the all-star game against other leagues. They'll often show us how much better we could have been if we hadn't allowed our victories to make us complacent.

• Wins shouldn't be important because they help us to avoid being stigmatized by losses. Losing shouldn't bear a stigma if we have practiced well and played with heart.

• Winning doesn't cleanse or redeem, despite the rhetoric we hear from sportswriters, professional coaches, and career players. To say "We need a win" is to overinflate the importance of sports, especially at the amateur level.

When you tune in to pro football next season, you're bound to hear an announcer say something like this: "The '49ers are expected to dominate today's game against the Packers. If they don't win by twenty points or more, they'll feel it's a loss." This is a perfect prescription for snatching defeat from the jaws of victory.

We need to be careful not to make the same mistake, which inadvertently transforms our victories into losses.

PART IX

Surviving Predictable Crises in Coaching

72.

Handling Boo-Boos and More Serious Injuries

THERE IS A short video on the subject of safety that is put out by Little League Baseball and the CNA Insurance Company. Irrespective of the sport you coach, I suggest you require all of your coaches to see it or something like it.

It runs about thirty minutes and covers everything from scrapes to fractures to life-threatening concussions. In a word, it scared me, by demonstrating what harms could happen during a game.

Outfielders can collide with each other. If their heads crash together, or if the impact to their bodies is severe enough, it could put someone into a coma, or worse. Less dramatic is the very real risk that kids run of developing heatstroke. Again, this can be life threatening unless they're cooled down and attended to quickly by paramedics or physicians.

If there is one thing I walked away with from the video, it's this: **Always have ice on hand.** If you don't have a refreshment stand that can be relied on to have ice available, take some from your fridge, put it into a small cooler, and carry it with you to practices and games. *Always* take ice.

In consecutive games one season, my daughter injured and then reinjured the same finger. We were able to stem the swelling because we had ice. A handy ice cube can also be used to cool down your players on sweltering days.

One more thing: Don't underestimate the scope of potential internal injuries. If there has been a major collision, don't rush to move the injured player or players, in the interest of resuming the game. You could inadvertently worsen someone's condition.

Whenever you're in doubt, summon the paramedics.

I urge you to carry a phone with you also, so that you can summon emergency personnel. This is especially necessary if you practice or play in a remote environment.

We've played away games at ballparks that are literally carved out of mountains. They're well-known habitats for rattlesnakes. There are no public telephones, and county services are miles away. If something happens, we have to be able to get help as soon as possible.

You should have a safety kit in your team's gear. Take it along to all events. Even if a kid needs only a Band-Aid, you'll feel better by being able to provide it instead of having to improvise.

Be especially alert whenever a player complains of dizziness, pain, headache, nausea, weakness, or restricted ability to move his or her muscles or body. These could be signs of trouble.

Remember too, that accidents will happen. Insurance companies know this. And some, thankfully, are helping coaches to prepare for them.

73.

When Kids Quit the Team

KIDS QUIT TEAMS for many reasons. Here are the top ten causes in no particular order:

1. They have competing extracurricular activities that get in the way of your practices and games. Why didn't they and their parents foresee these conflicts before signing up? Who knows?

2. They're afraid of failing. At the root of many departures, you'll find a lack of self-confidence. If they aren't messing up already, they fear they will when the game is on the line.

3. They're afraid of being injured.

4. They aren't getting along with their teammates. One of their teammates could be a bully.

5. Their schoolwork is below par, and their parents are pulling out all stops to do damage control.

6. They didn't want to be there to begin with. Mom or Dad talked the child into it, and predictably, the child was miserable.

7. Their parents are feuding with other parents. Because Dad is tempted to haul off and hit Billy's pop, Junior has just lost his ride to games and practices.

8. They thought they would be much better than they're turning out to be. Rather than confronting their lack of progress and working hard to improve, they'd prefer to quit. They may quietly decide to take up another sport next season.

9. Parents have imposed too much pressure to excel, and the kids resent it. Adolescents, particularly those who have shown promise

as athletes, often find quitting a good way of getting back at overbearing forebears.

10. And last but not least, they may quit because of *you.* If you don't give them enough playing time, or you assign them to a less favored position, or you "harshly" critique or reprimand them, these can all be used as quitting justifications.

Whenever a kid quits, it tends to become conspicuous, at least to the remaining players. Those who depart may make your job easier if they tell their friends why they split. At other times, however, they'll storm off and pout, or they'll simply fade away, which will put you on the spot.

One of my kids who was perennially late to games and practices showed up in the last inning of a game in which we were being trounced. Incensed because I wouldn't instantly change the lineup to suit this late-comer, the player declared, "I'm never coming back!"

The other players had already left the field, so they were clueless as to why this otherwise talented athlete was permanently absent. When they asked me about it, instead of being put on the defensive, I simply said that they were better off to ask their friend directly.

Generally, if you aren't given a suitable reason for someone's departure, I suggest you avoid the temptation to invent one. You can say, "I'm not sure, and he will be missed. But we'll find a way to get along, and I'm sure he wishes you well."

End of story. Even if we knew for certain that a kid was having a power struggle with his parents, we'd be way out of line to disclose this fact. It's much too private.

And that's the case with most of the reasons kids quit. Is it anyone's business that Emily's grades are tanking? Do we need to add fuel to the fire if a couple of parents are feuding?

Unless a kid is being bullied, which a coach should be able to see and correct immediately, most of the reasons kids leave the scene are not in our hands to manage. Understand that, and you'll quickly recover from their departure.

74.
Disciplining Your Players During Games

It was the top half of the last inning, and the visiting team was down by two runs. Bases were loaded, and the opposing pitcher couldn't find the strike zone.

The manager called time-out and sprinted up to confer with his hitter. "Take every pitch until she throws a strike," he instructed. Then, he double-checked to make sure his signal was understood. The hitter nodded her head.

She stepped back into the batter's box, and as instructed, she took the first two pitches. They missed the plate by a wide margin. Then, mysteriously, she swung at the third pitch, which was also well outside of the strike zone.

Reflexively, the manager boomed out, "That wasn't the sign!"

A man's voice responded from the bleachers, "Leave her alone!" Then, the batter's father stormed the field, charging in the direction of the manager at third base.

The umpire stopped him before any physical harm could be inflicted. The game resumed, and the batter let the next two pitches go by without swinging. She walked as the manager had predicted, forcing in a run.

Her team tied the game during that inning, only to lose it by a run during the home team's last time at bat. It was clear that her father's threatening behavior had had a chilling effect on the losing team. They might have won but for the altercation between the parent and the manager.

This sort of scene is becoming all too typical in kids' leagues. Parents, coaches, and players are having misunderstandings because there aren't clear guidelines for critiquing and disciplining players.

Was the manager acting properly when he publicly admonished his player for contravening an express instruction to not swing until the pitcher had thrown a strike? What was he trying to accomplish?

Here's what he said afterwards: "When you're a player, you have to follow directions. When you're given a sign, your team is depending on you to follow it. It can mean the difference between winning and losing. I told her right away, and publicly, that she blew it because I wanted her and everyone on the team to know that you just don't do that."

The father was equally adamant: "I don't want anybody yelling at my kid or disciplining her. That's my job."

So, who's right?

It's hard to say. If you believe that it is part of the role of a coach to be a disciplinarian and to keep players in line, then you might side with the manager—even if he was a little louder than he could have been under less pressured circumstances.

If you believe that coaches shouldn't discipline players or compel them to follow instructions, then you're going to arrive at a different judgment.

This topic is another one that you should cover, if at all possible, in advance in a meeting with your parents. Clear guideines should be established for everyone's behavior. The question of discipline shouldn't be answered through improvisation or impulsiveness on the part of coaches or parents.

75.
Obnoxious Opposing Coaches

EVERY NOW AND then, you can expect to encounter an obnoxious opposing coach.

Your counterpart could be hypercompetitive and question every close call the umpire or referee makes. He or she could implicitly or explicitly claim that you're cheating, or at least "bending the rules." The coach may treat players poorly by teasing them with sarcasm after they've blown a play.

And this person may do everything in his or her power to upset you and make you lose your cool.

When I was a new Little League manager, we had to play some practice games before the regular season. It so happened that the El Niño storms were ravaging southern California, and every day, the weather was touchy.

On the night before our second practice game, the rains came down without interruption. The next morning, there were still intermittent downpours. Our contest was scheduled for 12:45 that afternoon, and at 10:30, the heavens were still crying.

I phoned my players to inform them that the field couldn't possibly be safe enough by game time. But when I notified the league of my decision, the league's representative informed me that my opposing coach still wanted to play the game, and that he said if I didn't bring my team out in the rain, I'd "forfeit."

Well, that's a fighting word, if you ask me. Who but the wimpiest of souls ever wants to forfeit, right? Nonetheless, I stuck to my guns. I wasn't going to subject my kids to the palpable risk of injury.

Well, wonder of wonders, the skies cleared up by game time, and the temperature soared to about seventy-eight degrees. But the field was a mess. A sign had been posted by the city: the field was closed until further notice.

I *couldn't* have forfeited because the city had made my decision not to play irrelevant. But the opposing coach had accomplished his mission: to put a new manager on the defensive.

You can expect to encounter obnoxious opposing coaches. Just make sure to keep your cool. Don't let them throw you off your game plan or keep you from doing what you believe is in the best interests of your team.

76.

Dropping Kids from Teams

If you ever want to be called "the Coach from Hell," just drop a kid from your team.

I've done it, earning that appellation—and others, I'm sure, that I *didn't* hear about. It wasn't a happy event for the child, her parents, me, or my family.

It resulted from a clash that had occurred because this girl was missing numerous practices and games, which placed burdens on the team and the coaching staff. Instead of reforming her behavior, her parents insisted that I was wrong to require her to follow the rules.

At certain times, any leader can expect to be unpopular. If you can't handle this, you may want to reconsider the idea of coaching.

I suppose there are coaches who can function without having to drop kids from teams or perform other unpleasant tasks. This doesn't mean they aren't effective leaders, it simply means their leadership hasn't been *tested*. Sooner or later, yours will be. Trust me on this.

I know one fellow who decided to become a "lifetime" assistant coach because he wanted to avoid becoming a lightning rod for criticism. His idea was to let the manager or head coach take the heat, and he was up front about not wanting to be the point man in any conflict involving players or their parents.

Cowardly as his position may appear, he has a point. If your top priorities are peace and tranquility, you can avoid a lot of flack by not accepting the top coaching job if it is offered. You can thus remain mute when kids or their parents break the rules.

However, if you are in charge, and if you ever consider removing a kid from the roster, I suggest you do these things:

1. Make it clear to players and parents from the beginning of the season that certain infractions constitute "removable offenses."

Chronic absences could be one of them; theft of equipment would be another; bullying peers could be a third. Have a list.

2. If there's time, issue formal warnings to parents that these are unacceptable behaviors and require immediate cessation.

3. Notify the league of the specific problem with your player, and explain that removal is imminent.

4. If the offending behavior isn't cured, notify the parent or parents that the child has been removed from the roster.

Note that removal has financial ramifications as well. In some leagues, it costs $100 or more for a child to sign up for a team. The league should establish a league procedure for issuing a refund or a pro rata rebate after uniforms and equipment have been returned in decent condition.

In some cases, removal from a team may not require dropping a kid from the league. A "trade" might be accomplished between teams, to the relative advantage of both. However, be alert to the potential for perpetuating hard feelings. You may determine that a trade won't be advantageous in the short or long run, and it may set a dangerous precedent in which kids who aren't happy start insisting upon being traded.

Removing kids from a team isn't enjoyable or popular, but it is necessary in certain circumstances. Don't be reluctant to use this tool when it's called for.

77.
How to Defuse Potentially Violent Situations

IN MY LAST year of graduate school, I needed something to take my mind off of my career and my studies. So, I signed up for a softball league.

My team consisted of other working people, and they were pleasant enough . . . until one evening when mayhem broke loose.

Two of our players were cousins, and the mom of one of them was a fixture at practices and games. Apparently, she criticized her nephew a little too harshly when he was taking batting practice, and he charged the stands.

Suddenly, a fight erupted. The aunt, who had to be in her fifties, was taking on all comers, including her twenty-something nephew.

That altercation ended our season. We were light on personnel to begin with, and after that bizarre episode, the cousins refused to play with each other. So, we couldn't field enough players.

I couldn't imagine then why a fight broke out, but now, having coached kids' sports, I have come to expect frayed emotions, parental outbursts, and potential violence.

As a coach, what can you do if you believe a hostile episode is imminent? Assuming you're between innings, or the game has already concluded and your attention isn't riveted to the playing field, you can try one or more of these strategies:

• Distract the troubled person: Strike up a conversation about something irrelevant to this particular game and set of circumstances.

• Compliment the person: If you like his car, say so. Get him to talk about his barber, after mentioning that you're looking for a new one, and he always looks sharp.

- Use humor: Tell him a joke, or mention something funny that you knew he'd get a kick out of. It doesn't matter if it's a bad joke, or hokey or silly. If you can evoke a laugh, you'll be halfway home in calming him down.

- Ask him a question and pay close attention to the answer: "Did I hear it right that you're an animator? That has always fascinated me."

- If the person is blaming you or someone else, don't contradict him. Instead, try, "Well, I respect your opinion about that." Then, carry on with whatever else you were doing.

- If appropriate, agree and accept blame or responsibility: Say, "You're right—I blew it. I'm sorry about that."

- If you must make something clear, don't flatly interrupt. Instead, use transition phrases, which are quick conversational bridges. For example, "Well, I understand that . . ."; "Well I appreciate that . . ."; "Well, I'd be surprised if you were at this point . . ."; "Well, I know what you mean . . . ."
After using any of these qualifiers, you can go on to state the point that you need to make, knowing that it will be more favorably received than if you had just blurted it out in an argumentative way.

- Postpone the discussion if you think this strategy will provide a cooling off period. Say, for instance, "I'd like to talk about this with you. Can we get together after the game, following the team meeting?" By agreeing to a time and place, you'll be starting to cooperate, which can be built upon later when you get together.

- If you must interact with the person, try to have another coach or an umpire or referee at your side: People tend to be less hostile when they feel their comments and behaviors are being audited by multiple people.

- One of the best ways to avoid a fight is to walk away. This can be hard to do if you feel there is an important principle at stake, or if you feel you have been personally criticized, but remember the adage from childhood—"Sticks and stones may break my bones, but names will never hurt me."

Your coaching career may never be marred by overt hostilities. I certainly hope this is the case. But it would be wise to be prepared for anything.

78.

How Can You Fire a Volunteer?

RUBEN HAS JUST taken over as manager of the Green Dragons. Although he hasn't coached softball before, he has coached soccer and basketball. Having been a good baseball player in his younger years, he knows the game.

In a short time, he has whipped the team into shape. They've won their first three games, but he has already had a major, public argument with a parent about getting his kid to practices on time.

During games, Coach Ruben is very vocal and emotionally involved. Unlike a number of other coaches, he angers easily when opposing coaches try to "pull fast ones" on him. He also breaks certain traditions. For example, he's constantly changing the lineup to give kids of all ages a chance to play various positions.

His lineup changes have angered the parents of eleven- and twelve-year-olds who believe that their kids should be given seniority and be entitled to play their positions without interruption. Moreover, instead of always starting the older players, he'll occasionally allow the nine- and ten-year-olds to start games and then bring in the older players as substitutes.

A few parents have been lobbying to get Ruben removed from the coaching staff. Because his child is only nine, he is scheduled to manage the team for another three years after this season ends. The disgruntled parents have approached you, as a fellow parent, with their complaints and have asked for your support.

What should you do? What can be done?

Occasionally, coaches seem to be lightning rods for criticism. For various reasons, they may not get along with the players, their fellow parents, officials, the league, or other coaches, for that matter.

Let's look at this situation with Ruben. Are there grounds for making him retire from his managerial duties? What, exactly, has Ruben done?

1. He has shown more emotion during games than other managers show.

2. He clashes with other managers when he perceives they're out of line.

3. He rotates playing positions instead of establishing permanent positions.

4. Occasionally, he starts younger players at the beginning of games, which makes older players have to wait for their turn to enter games.

5. He has publicly criticized a parent.

6. In doing these things, he has violated unwritten "rules" or traditions.

Does any one of these acts justify his removal? Even taken together as a whole, are they so troubling that they make his termination desirable?

After all, it's a little awkward to try to "fire" a volunteer, especially one who hasn't done anything illegal or unethical. Clearly, Ruben hasn't done anything this extreme, but a number of parents still don't like this newcomer.

My belief is that Ruben shouldn't be removed at this time. A better recourse is for someone to address the situation with him directly and delicately:

- He can be asked to have an informal meeting with the other coaches on the team. They can discuss some of the traditions he seems to have violated. Moreover, they can fill him in on the "etiquette" involved in communicating with parents and opposing coaches. If he and opposing coaches have some ill will toward each other, his colleagues can step into his shoes to handle new issues that arise during games.

- A league official can offer to buy him a cup of coffee and then initiate the same discussion as just described. Ideally, before the season began, Ruben would have been briefed about some of the things to watch out for. But in this case, we're assuming he wasn't.

- A parent who feels at least "neutral" about Ruben could chat with him.

Once he has been given feedback, if his behavior worsens, there may be grounds for sanctioning him further.

The politics involved in kids' sports can be painful. We can easily forget that we're mainly there to help children have fun, grow, and develop certain positive social and leadership skills. Even if Ruben and coaches like him aren't deserving of removal, it becomes a major distraction for them and for the players if their performance is being constantly criticized.

Consequently, those who lobby for removal have a good chance of having their way sooner or later. Unfortunately, this can not only impede the progress of new coaches but also discourage other parents from coming forward to volunteer.

So, what's the bottom line in "firing" volunteers? It's a lot like firing an employee:

1. You put the person on notice regarding the offensive conduct.

2. You allow time for the person to modify his or her behavior.

3. If improvement isn't forthcoming, or if the conduct worsens, you can ask for a resignation or ask the league to remove the person.

PART X

When to Scale Back or Bow Out of Coaching

79.
Ten Sure Signs That You're Getting Too Involved

COACHING IS A lot of fun if you just relax and remind yourself that you aren't playing for money, for prestige, or for any number of other reasons. If you're not having enough fun, and it seems like a thankless job, you may have started to get too involved.

Here are ten signs that you've stepped into "foul" territory:

1. You'd rather make out a lineup card than talk with your spouse or best friend. I know whereof I speak. I would commit more than an hour to making out the lineup before games. How come it took so long? I overstrategized, taking into account whether my pitcher had a good or bad outing during the last game, and whether my first-string catcher needed a break. I wasted a lot of paper making change after change when I could have done the lineups in ten minutes, maximum.

If you tinker too much with any strategic element of your game, you're just plain overthinking.

2. You react defensively to any comment that a young person makes about your coaching decisions. Kids will say nearly anything if you listen to them long enough. Sometimes, my daughter will insult me just for the heck of it. "Hey Dad, you've got a double chin!"—that's a frequent wisecrack right now. So, be prepared for your players to second-guess your decisions. "Gee, Coach, we should have kept Heidi playing forward!" is something you can expect to hear.

Once, I was standing in the dugout, assigning the game's positions, and one girl heard that she was going to be in right field. She didn't say anything, really. She simply *kicked me!*

It was reflexive, and in its way, it was charming. I felt like "family." I was surprised, so I laughed and asked her: "Did you just *kick* me?" She denied it, and I let it pass without further comment.

3. You can't put a loss behind you within two hours. Actually, two whole hours is a long time to stew over a defeat. I should suggest you get over it in ten minutes, but this won't give you enough time to replay the game in your mind. After two hours, however, you're beating yourself up too much, or blaming somebody else far too intensely. Let it go!

4. You haven't played half of this year's games and are already worried about who you'll be starting on opening day next year. This is a waste of a strategic mind. If you're really into long-term planning, why not work with NASA on the Jupiter mission instead?

5. You start thinking that the game is in *your* hands to win or to lose. I've fallen into this trap more than once. It's an ego trip to think that you can affect enough variables on the field or the playing court to tip the scales. Of course, coaches have an impact, but once the game has begun, winning and losing are in the hands of your players, your opponents, and numerous unforeseen variables such as injuries and inconsistent officiating.

6. You lose patience with your own child and start wishing he or she were on another team. Well, you don't really wish that. You're just a little impatient because you have a dual role as a mom or dad and as a coach. You can feel that team interests come before those of your child, but this is a mistake. Teams come and go. Your family will be a part of your life forever.

7. You're more concerned about avenging a loss than developing your players' abilities. I have to admit that I've relished beating certain teams. Not because I had anything against their players or parents, but because I've felt that their coaches were bozos. Whenever this kind of destructively competitive fervor is awakened in you—beware. You'll make expedient decisions that might win the game and beat that opposing coach but also compromise the development of your players.

For example, you might remove a player who is starting to slip in effectiveness. Although your team is comfortably ahead, you rationalize doing this for defensive reasons.

But your action would deny your player a chance to work through the doldrums and to recover his or her poise. *That* could be a more significant contribution as a coach than winning a particular game. If players learn to work their way out of trouble, that lesson could raise the level of their play for the remainder of the season and for the rest of their lives.

Balance the significance of that achievement against the temporary ego surge that you'll have by besting another coach, obnoxious as the person may be.

8. Parents, opponents, umpires, or league officials start looking like "the enemy." This is a sure sign that you're burning out. Look in the mirror. There's your enemy.

9. You start losing your sense of humor. I suppose this applies to nearly any activity. If you can't step back and put a smile on your face from time to time, you're living in a two-dimensional world. Lighten up!

10. Someone remarks, "Hey—it's only a game," and you think he should have his head examined. It is just a game. When it takes on symbolic importance and becomes the vehicle through which you're going to demonstrate your coaching ability or your sports genius, you're doomed.

80.
Learn to Delegate to Make the Burden Lighter

ONE OF THE main reasons people volunteer is to get involved in something significant. By being thoroughly engrossed in an activity, we can enter that nearly blissful state where we lose ourselves and find ourselves at the same time.

But we have to limit our involvement for practical reasons. There isn't time to become a twenty-four-hour-a-day soccer coach. Even if there were, making such a commitment wouldn't necessarily be a good thing for us or for the players. We could lose perspective and become overly involved from an emotional standpoint.

How can we set limits, then, and stick to them, when there are so many things that need to be done? Well, we just have to do what effective business managers learn to do. They delegate.

As involved adults, we need to depend on the contributions of other parents and coaches to make this engine that is our team a smoothly running one.

Here are four of the "unofficial" roles that need to be filled:

1. **The unofficial team parent:** a person who operates in the shadow of the official one. As explained in Part II, this person stays in touch with the real TP to assure that snack schedules are known and that everyone has been called about scheduling, team photos, and other functions.

2. **The unofficial practice coach:** the parent who stays to watch kids practice. If this person is just sitting on the sidelines, you're not delegating effectively! Get the onlooker involved in doing something

important: leading a drill or assisting during one, or handing out or collecting equipment.

3. **The unofficial game coach:** could be the same person who helps during practices or somebody different. It doesn't matter. When your official coaches don't show up, or when they're occupied on the sidelines warming up replacement pitchers, your unofficial game coach takes over.

4. **Your sounding board:** a parent who doesn't do any of the above. But just as important is what he or she will do for you and for the team. Your sounding board is the person to whom you can turn in order to discuss strategy and to tap into the pipeline of parental and players' feelings and attitudes.

Don't even think of becoming an island unto yourself, or con yourself into believing you can do everything—or that it's easier if you do. It isn't.

Limit your involvement by getting other parents involved. That way, they'll have more fun, and you don't have to be everything to everybody.

81.

When Removing Yourself
from a Game Is a Good Idea

BEFORE YOU BECOME a coach, you may want to serve as a helper to the official coaches. I did it, and it led to some interesting insights and experiences.

During practices, I'd fill in at positions when kids were absent. I'd also gather bats and balls and generally be a gofer for the regular coaches. During games, I'd often coach at third base. In general, I'd allow myself to be pointed in the direction in which I was needed. Being a helper enabled me to learn the ropes of coaching from a comfortable distance.

One season, the manager of our team and one of his coaches decided that they were not going to come to one of the games. They had been feuding with the opposing coaches, and this was an expression of protest.

When I heard about their plan, I was alarmed. I figured, if they weren't going to be there, we might have to forfeit the game, which I thought would be unfair to the kids. Because I had no history with the opposing coaches, I volunteered to be a "coach for a day," and it was agreed that the game would go on as scheduled. I'd be at the helm, along with the team's third coach.

That day, I did everything I could to appear gracious and generous with our opponents. They responded in kind, and we all had a lot of fun.

As it turned out, our team won by the widest margin we had achieved that season. After that, we went on to defeat this rival two additional times during the season, which transformed a long losing spell into a winning streak.

By bowing out of that one game, our manager and coach actually did something very constructive—though it may have been inadvertent. They enabled us to focus on the game instead of being distracted by our opposing coaches' personalities. By doing this, we made the right moves and had a great time.

As a business consultant, I have seen situations in which managers just don't know how to get out of their own way. They become part of the problem instead of facilitating a solution. In most cases, they didn't have the wisdom or the imagination to remove themselves from the scene so others could set things straight.

As a coach, you'll find that periodically disengaging from games is a constructive move. By removing yourself, you'll enable other parents and helpers to step up in your place. They'll grow from the experience, and this small act will enable you to strengthen your entire coaching staff.

Plus, you'll get the satisfaction of knowing that there are various ways to win. One of the best is by voluntarily restraining yourself.

82.

Your Comments Can Have Long-Lasting Impact

THE AMOUNT OF clout a coach can have in a young person's life is awesome. This fact can be energizing as well as humbling.

One of my teams was having a so-so year, but one girl stood out. Just eleven, she had the abilities and the swagger of a veteran ballplayer. When we were on the field, she seemed to breathe in the experience through every pore. She was immersed in the sport and was a pleasure to be around.

I'd have her warm up with shy kids and with those who hadn't yet blossomed. I knew that her enthusiasm would rub off on them, and she never let me down. One day, I realized that this player had to be told that she was the real thing—that she had the whole package. I felt that something might get her down at some point, a bad coach, or a parent with a careless comment, and I wanted to inoculate her against anything that would diminish her forward momentum.

So, I let her know: I said, "You have the heart of a champion." I wanted her to hear these words when the going got tough, in sports or in life, long after she had hung up her glove.

When I was twelve or thirteen, one of my coaches gave me a lecture about the importance of determination. He said that quitting—not giving 100 percent all of the time—is a disease. Never, ever, ever, *ever* quit, he admonished.

I accepted his message with the earnestness with which he issued it, but I think I went overboard in trying to fit this credo into my life. Decades later, as a businessperson, I found I was super-reluctant to ever quit on a losing product or give up on people who were underperforming.

Then, I found this prescription being contradicted in a class with management guru Peter Drucker. He urged us to use what he calls "systematic abandonment." This is a process of relentlessly giving up on products and services (and probably, people) that aren't pulling their weight.

This seemed almost completely alien to me, probably because of the "Never Quit" lecture my old coach had given me. Finally, I reconciled the two positions, which I determined were both too extreme.

Likewise, as coaches, we need to recognize that our players will long remember what we've told them. So, let's make sure it's always upbeat and helps them to feel that they're champions. If you aren't comfortable with the responsibility that this influence confers, it's a good reason to avoid coaching.

83.
Periodically, Give Your Kids a Breather from Coach Mom and Coach Dad

WHY DO MOST kids relish the chance to go away to camp for at least a few days? It gives them an opportunity to be away from Mom and Dad. They can let down their hair. Though they have to report to counselors, it isn't the same as having to please one's parents.

Kids also need a chance to enjoy at least some sports without having to answer to us as coaches. One year, I made the mistake of coaching three sports in a row: soccer, basketball, and then baseball. I think it would have been better for my daughter and for me if I had allowed a little more downtime between coaching assignments.

Here's why:

1. It's tough being a coach's child. You're almost always onstage. If you goof off, it's conspicuous. It also sends a message to other players that it's OK. So, your behavior is likely to be more guarded and a little more serious than that of others.

Being a role model can be fun if you aspire to that status. Having it thrust upon you because of who your mom or dad is—well, that's a different story.

2. If an ordinary coach seems to be disappointed in your performance on the court or playing field, it's irritating, but you'll probably get over it. If your mom or dad seems disappointed, it can feel devastating. You might be concerned that you'll lose their affection. This emotional double whammy is hard on coaches' kids.

3. Most coaches are going to be tougher on their kids than on the rest of the team. They don't want to show favoritism toward their own, so they err in the other direction. As an assistant soccer coach, I had to urge the head coach to play his daughter as a forward, despite the fact that she was one of the most qualified individuals who could be assigned to that position. If I hadn't interceded on her behalf, she would have languished where she was playing and wouldn't have contributed nearly as much to the team.

Some parents may feel that it isn't necessary to take a break from coaching one's kids. They may feel indispensable to the team, and in fact, they could be superb leaders. But they shouldn't forget that the most important reason they're coaching is to help their kids to have a rich and well-rounded life.

Sometimes, we should put ourselves on the bench and take a season or two off. Though they may not say a peep, your kids will be grateful that you were a smart enough parent to give them a breather from Coach Mom or Coach Dad.

84.
The "Genius" in Rotating Managers

HAVE YOU EVER noticed how some politicians suddenly seem to improve when they have publicly announced that they're not running for reelection?

They try to engineer bipartisan support. They attempt to enact ambitious legislation. They feel they don't have to worry about electoral consequences, so they make an effort to rise above petty politics and serve the greater good.

I think we should impose "term limits" on head coaches and managers of kids' teams. They should "retire" from or rotate out of these roles after each season. They might still coach after a year of service, but not in the top spot. Here are my reasons:

1. The "politics" of coaching can be brutal and can take a toll on the most patient of us. Dealing with the same batch of parents for several years is too much to ask from an average human being. Frayed emotions can worsen from season to season, causing the fabric of any team to unravel.

2. Managers need to make unpopular decisions. They're easier to make and to accept if everyone knows that the head person is going to step down at the end of the season. If one manager failed to see the potential in a given player, his or her successor may decide to reverse that error.

3. When the manager's role is shifted to other coaches on the staff, everyone gets a chance to call the shots, and to have a meaningful impact upon strategy. This is empowering and skill building, and it can enrich a number of lives. Why should only one person get that kind of satisfaction from being involved?

4. Rotations encourage more parents to become active. Knowing they'll get a chance to lead the team, more folks will have a reward to which they can look forward, so they'll come aboard in greater numbers.

5. Rotations encourage us to remember that these sports leagues exist to help our kids to develop. If we really want a career in coaching, we should create a real one and not live out this fantasy through our kids' teams.

6. "Bad" managers are automatically let go every year when the position rotates. There is no overt bloodletting. They simply move on without bearing any stigma, and with fewer hard feelings.

Just as there are term limits in political life, they make sense in coaching as well. Try rotating the position of head coach or manager, and I think you and your team will appreciate the "genius" in it.

85.
When Should You Resign from Coaching?

IF YOU WERE a manager in a corporation, what would make you consider resigning from your position? As I see it, seven things might prompt you to consider withdrawing:

1. Your boss doesn't support you by backing up your decisions.

2. The people who report to you seem to take exception to your overall management style.

3. You can't seem to get along with certain big customers with whom you have to deal in the normal course of business.

4. You don't feel you are generating the right levels of productivity from your people.

5. The rewards you receive turn out to be fewer or less valuable than the ones you expected.

6. You felt happier before you accepted the position.

7. You start dreading the idea of coming to work each day.

Any of these negatives could induce you to consider leaving your post. The same factors should be taken into account when determining if you would be well advised to resign from coaching. Let's consider them in order:

1. You don't have a "boss" as such when you coach, but you do have to answer to your league. If the officials there won't support you when it comes to backing your decisions, then you have a problem.

Let's say you have a player who has signed up to play a competing sport. ("Encroachment" of other sports is discussed in #88 in Part XI.) He can't attend both your games and the others. You need to have your players present for practices and games, and you feel that he should be dropped from the roster so that the ones who do show up regularly can have more playing time. If you present this idea to the league, and they equivocate or contend that you're making a big thing out of nothing, you're going to be frustrated in doing your duty.

2. The "people who report to you" are your players. If you just don't click—let's say you're too authoritarian and they've been used to permissiveness—then you're going to be in trouble. You'll try to press harder, and they'll resist more and more.

You're not going to change, nor will they. You might want to apply your leadership skills to a group and to an activity in which they'll be more fitting.

3. You also don't have to deal with customers as such in kids' sports, but you must get along with parents. You'll need to have goodwill between you. One parent's ire is tolerable, but if a large contingent—say a fourth or a third—of your team's parents don't like you, you may want to cash in your chips while you still have some left.

4. If you can't get your players to do reasonably well, you could be a poor fit for coaching. Recognize it, and try to improve. Reach out to experienced coaches for guidance. Use their drills and approaches. If nothing works, pass the baton to another coach who might be more effective.

5. Coaching can look great from the outside. You seem to get to use your sports savvy and have a lot of fun. But a tremendous amount of hard work is involved. If you find that coaching is a far cry from what you thought it would be, you might want to pull out.

6. A few elections ago, a presidential candidate asked the electorate to consider this basic question: "Are you better off today than you were four years ago?"

Ask yourself: Are you happier coaching than you were when you were merely an interested parent? If you can't be certain, or if your answer is negative, you're probably better off cheering from the bleachers.

7. Are you dreading the next practice or game or league meeting? You could be burning out. Face facts, and reassess your involvement.

If you do decide to pass the responsibility to others, there's one thing your own kid will regain. It's your undivided attention, and this may be more rewarding for both of you than coaching ever was.

PART XI

How Can We Improve the Sports Experience?

86.

Should Nine-Year-Olds Be Playing Against Twelve-Year-Olds?

WHEN I PLAYED in Little League, I had to face a scary pitcher. Rob was head and shoulders above the rest of us in physical stature as well as pitching ability. Although he was twelve and I was eleven, the gulf between us was much greater than a single year.

Not only was he bigger and stronger, but he was also already *shaving*, for goshsakes! His fastball looked like a major leaguer's, and it took a lot of courage simply to enter the batter's box when he was on the mound.

One fateful day, I stepped up to bat left-handed. I figured if I could just chip a shot past third base, I'd be lucky. As it turned out, the ball nearly took a chip out of me.

Out of my knee, that is. I was hit by one of Rob's cannonballs and I instantly entered a new world of pain. My knee swelled immediately, and I was definitely out of the game. Had the ball hit a slightly different location, I might have been out for the season.

How hard was that ball thrown? Let me put it this way: for weeks, I could see a clear impression of the "seams" of the ball on my bruised knee.

After my mishap, parents expressed concerns that Rob would permanently maim somebody, or worse. Rumors circulated that he was really older and was masquerading as a twelve-year-old. Others rushed to his aid, saying, "Heck, he's only twelve, and he has a right to play."

Of course, he did have a right to play. But my experience with Rob raises a more pertinent question, which, as a coach, I've heard from parents: Should twelve-year-olds be in the same league as those who are only nine?

The physical differences between these age-groups can be extreme. In terms of height alone, a four-footer could be squaring off against a six-footer. This dramatically increases the potential severity of injuries.

I don't know about you, but I cringe each time I see a giant player sliding into a peewee. In soccer, a powerful kick to a small player's shin can easily break bone, despite the fact that players are required to wear shin guards.

Some Little Leagues have two divisions: one for nine- and ten-year-olds, and a separate one for eleven- and twelve-year-olds. This makes a lot of sense. Not only are the players developmentally closer to each other, but they also share similar attitudes as preteens.

Coaches also have an easier job under this arrangement because there aren't such great disparities in playing abilities. They can spend time covering either basics or advanced techniques without feeling that they're moving too quickly for the junior set or too slowly for the more experienced and more skilled.

Some leagues argue that they don't have enough players to go around; if they were to split kids into more age-groups, they'd have to get by with fewer teams. I understand this concern, but I still think it's worth a try.

I'd rather see kids playing in a more appropriate peer group than competing against a greater variety of teams. Moreover, leagues can always agree with neighboring cities and towns to occasionally play each other's teams, or even to form a regional league.

I recovered from Rob's bullet. In fact, I came up against him the same year. That time, I lined a shot up the middle into center field for a clean hit.

The ball missed *his* knee by about six inches.

87.

Are We a Farm Team for the Majors?

WHEN I WAS twelve, I had a banner year in Little League.

I led the league in batting with a .582 average and barely missed being crowned the home run king. The player who earned that distinction had just one more homer than I did. (To make things worse, as a fielder, he "robbed" me of an opening-day homer.) I was captain of my team and of our league's all-star team. I suppose you might say I had an ideal season.

At the end of the year, my father disclosed that he had already talked to scouts from the major leagues, who had advised him to keep me in baseball. After he mentioned that, I felt a lot of pressure. Adolescence was kicking in, and my interests turned to girls and to rebellion. Baseball seemed, suddenly, to be on a back burner, and the more my dad pushed me to excel, the cooler I got about complying.

I felt that his dreams of glory were taking the place of mine.

Whenever he'd introduce me to his business associates, I'd be referred to as "the ballplayer." I liked this at first because it gave me special stature while distinguishing me from my older brother and sister, but as I matured, I came to resent it. I was developing various interests that had nothing to do with baseball. I retreated from my sport, creating a gulf between dad and myself.

After a few years away from the game, I started hearing "When are you going back to baseball?" I did return to play varsity ball during my senior year in high school, and then I played summer ball with a division of a major-league team.

But my heart wasn't in it. While some of my teammates were signing with pro teams, I was wondering what I was really going to do with my life.

Parents and coaches can push kids too far, too fast. Don't fall into this trap. Let your kid's sport be as much fun as it can be, for as long as possible. If you see parents imposing their dreams upon their kids, gently advise them to back off.

88.

Fighting the Encroachment of Other Sports

I SUFFERED THROUGH the worst season of my volunteer-coaching career because of the encroachment of competing sports. Let me set the scene for you before I tell you how this happened.

When I was growing up, there were three primary sports in America: football, basketball, and baseball. As the leaves of autumn fell, we knew in our bones that we'd soon be sloshing through them in reverie with a "pigskin" clutched in our icy hands.

Then, as winter howled, we'd move indoors to play basketball, which would end about the time of the spring thaw. Then, with sunshine popping through the clouds, we'd grab our bats and gloves and head out onto the playgrounds and baseball diamonds.

Every sport had its place, and the natural order of things was perfect if you were drawn to play all three, as I was. Before the official start of every sport, there were at least a few weeks of time for practicing and working dormant muscles into shape. No coach had to worry that, barring injuries, his or her players would be unavailable for their sports when the proper time rolled around.

But this is changing. Two trends have altered the neat ecology we once knew.

First, professional sports teams have proliferated, and their changing schedules are impacting those of amateur and youth leagues. Major-league sports franchises are not only esconced in large cities but are also insinuating themselves into smaller markets. With more teams come more games, including more play-offs at season's end. This means that seasons are lasting much longer—at least several weeks, and in some cases, a few months longer.

Baseball's World Series used to be played during the first week of the new school year, as I recall. This was in early September. Now we're lucky to have the Fall Classic end by the time November begins. Baseball blasts through the start of the football season, which has been backed up to August and which now runs nearly smack into February, with the Super Bowl being pushed later and later into January.

The other trend comes from individual sports, such as soccer, which is becoming a year-round activity, especially among kids. In California, there is one soccer season that extends from August through November; play-offs and all-star activities can reach into January, however. But then, there is a second season: Spring soccer starts up in February and moves into early summer.

With soccer, we are facing the first highly organized, year-round sport. It constitutes more than a threat to tradition, as it boldly encroaches upon other sports. It is going to force our kids to "specialize" in certain sports at earlier and earlier ages. And by forcing them to specialize, it will narrow their span of interests and potential sources of enjoyment.

Coaching will become more difficult. I've already seen this in Little League baseball, where some parents are signing up their kids for sports that have conflicting schedules.

You might wonder what a kid will do if he or she has a soccer commitment at the same time as a baseball game. Obviously, one sport will have to "give," and as a coach, you hope it won't be yours. What if two or more of your better players happen to be talented baseball and soccer players? Won't their absences prejudice your team's chances of winning?

How can you handle the interruptions and lack of predictability and consistency that these conflicts will inflict upon your team? I've had to handle these issues, and I have to tell you, they're creating significant problems.

I urge you to do what you can to fight the encroachment of expansionary sports schedules. They're more than an inconvenience; they're going to threaten our very ability to keep these important activities organized and operating smoothly for everyone's benefit.

Every sport may have to abbreviate its season to restore the order and balance that we once had. But this is a small concession to make to provide our kids with a number of enjoyable options to pursue.

89.
Establishing Codes of Conduct

IMAGINE DRIVING A car in an environment in which there are no traffic laws. Someone who doesn't like the way you drive could haul you into court, and a judge would then decide if you had done something unlawful. There would be no way that you could know in advance what was expected of you, nor what is permitted and what is prohibited.

This would be a very uncivilized way of governing conduct, don't you agree? Yet this is the state of the art in many kids' sports. Parents, coaches, and kids can make life very difficult for others and yet not be compelled to change their behavior. This should be addressed.

For example, during one game, when my team was rallying to tie the score in the last inning, a parent stormed the field to confront me about one of my coaching decisions. The umpire had to restrain this fellow and eject him from the playing area.

I asked the league whether we had any sanctions that could be levied against parents. "No, we don't—but you could write some up" was the lame reply I received. Well, let's do that, taking the field-storming incident as the offending event.

Everyone should be agreed that no occasion, apart from one's child having possibly sustained a major injury, justifies a parent's rushing onto a court or playing field. Such behavior not only interrupts the game but also intimidates players, coaches, and other parents. It also promotes retaliation. A coach who felt truly threatened could haul off and hit the threatening parent, or vice versa.

How should this offender be treated? There are several possible remedies:

• The parent can be "officially warned" by the league. Preferably, this would be done orally as well as in writing.

• The parent can be prevented from attending a game or two.

- The parent can be fined. A hundred or two hundred dollars might get the offender's attention and make him or her hesitant to obstruct a game again.

- If the conduct is a continuing problem, the offender can be banned for the remainder of the season.

- The offender's child can be dropped from the team and from the league.

You may agree or disagree with this approach, but I hope you'll agree with the need to have definite sanctions that are known to all parents and coaches.

Verbal conduct is more difficult to regulate. For instance, you'd probably agree with me that coaches shouldn't swear when addressing their players. It's uncivilized, and we don't want our kids to emulate it.

However, imagine this scenario: A heated basketball game is under way, and at the last second, the opposing team sinks a basket and wins. A frustrated parent exclaims, "Damn!" Should the parent be punished for using this word?

At what point does the parent's right to free speech conflict with your league's rules? Let's say the court is in a public park—no law has been broken, has it?

Some behaviors are easier to sanction than others. We move into a murky area when we try to regulate merely obnoxious behavior, whether it is manifested by players, parents, or coaches.

When you consider drafting a specific code of conduct, try to keep these caveats in mind:

- Clarity counts. Carefully and narrowly define the behaviors that are punishable.

- Don't try to develop a code that requires people to be "nice" or to be "pleasant."

- Provide incremental sanctions. First, provide a warning. Next, take away a privilege. Finally, allow a remedy that is a permanent punishment, making it impossible to be a chronic offender.

- Ask yourself if anyone could "accidentally" violate a rule and be subjected to a punishment that is too extreme. Redraft or reconsider any rule that you think can be too easily broken or disregarded.

- Avoid legislating anything that is traditionally a part of the sports experience. Crowds cheer and coaches yell. Sometimes the cheers are jeers, and yelling becomes shrieking. Trying to distinguish between these behaviors is difficult, if not impossible. Moreover, what constitutes a yell or a shriek will be interpreted differently by different people.

Don't put yourself into the position of making too many judgment calls. Everyone who is involved with kids' sports can't intuitively do the right thing all the time. Let's give our colleagues and friends a hand by offering some reasonable guidelines that can make the experience a more consistently positive one.

90.
Everyone's a Winner When We Don't Keep Score

IT'S THE LAST inning, and your team is behind by one run. Bases are loaded. You've noticed that the opposing pitcher is losing control, falling behind in the count. You consider your options.

If you allow your hitter to swing away, it's possible he'll strike out and end the game. If you put the take sign on—at least until the pitcher has thrown one strike—you'll have a good chance of your player drawing a walk and evening the score.

It's a big thrill for a kid to come up in a pressure situation like this and to pull through with a timely, game-winning hit. On the other hand, your team hasn't been winning lately, and it would be nice to at least tie this one. Plus, if your hitter strikes out, the child could feel bad for a long time.

What do you do? One strategy will get you closer to a tie, and the other, more risky strategy might get you the win . . .

This is more than a strategic question, as you might sense. It boils down to what winning is all about. Most people would define winning as having a better score than your opponent in the record book by the time a game ends. But *winning* is about much more than outscoring another team.

Its meaning goes deeper than that, particularly in our country. In the movie *Patton*, the general expresses his view in an emphatic speech before his troops. He declares: "Americans love a winner and simply won't tolerate a loser!"

This sentiment was echoed years later in a quote attributed to the revered Green Bay Packer coach Vince Lombardi: "Winning isn't everything; it's the *only* thing."

Just how important is winning? Your players, their parents, the league, and your fellow coaches will have their own answers, secreted away in their hearts and minds. As with most things involved in coaching, I think we should flesh out these concepts and come to terms with them. Your ideas about winning will definitely inform your coaching style. They'll also have a mighty impact on the satisfaction that various people will derive from the sport.

THE Y-WINNERS BASKETBALL PROGRAM

Patton and Lombardi expressed a widely held view about winning, but it certainly isn't the only one available. In fact, some leagues are purposely trying to redefine what winning is, so that kids' sports will be more enjoyable and less punitive.

The YMCA sponsors a basketball program called Y-Winners that is noteworthy in many respects. Built upon the concept of teaching positive values as well as athletic mechanics, it endeavors to develop kids as people.

Perhaps the most significant feature of this program is the fact that games are not scored. You won't see big numbers posted on a neon scoreboard at soccer matches or basketball games. In most cases, the scoreboard won't even be turned on unless it has a game clock.

The philosophy behind Y-Winners is that too much emphasis is placed on winning in kids' sports. If we remove scoring, we'll have a chance to make every participant *feel* like a winner.

Does it work? I can tell you from having coached in Y-Winners that a number of parents think so. After the last season, one of the moms thanked me. She said she had been reluctant to put her daughter into a sports program, but after Y-Winners, she was happy she did. The emphasis we placed on teamwork, skill development, and having a good time paid off in some very positive experiences and memories for her third-grader. Mom loved the fact that games weren't scored.

When you coach in a nonscoring atmosphere, several things are affected. First, you'll find that some players feel that something is missing. They'll ask, "What's the score?" or "Who won?" and they may seem a little disoriented to hear, "Everybody won!" But they get used to it.

I've discovered that I invest far less time trying to beat the opposing team, and far more time in developing my own. Instead of trying to determine where opponents are in the standings and what their probable strategies will be, I work on my game plan and adjust to the other team as our games proceed.

There's also a lot less stress in unscored games. The players have a rough idea about who is sinking the majority of their shots, but they are in the dark when it comes to any final statistics.

Intensely competitive parents and their children may not adjust very well to a system that doesn't encourage "stars" to develop. After all, if you're not scoring, how can you definitively say which player is better than another, and therefore, who is deserving of additional laurels?

It took me a little while to adjust. I coached in my first Y-Winners program immediately after having coached a soccer team to a series of victories and a championship. I had pulled out all the stops to win, and through the efforts of my fellow coaches and the team, we prevailed.

When I hit a program in which scoring was not going to be part of the picture, I had to question what I valued about coaching. Was I hooked on the excitement of never knowing whether a game would lead us to victory or defeat? Would I miss watching the standings to see where we ranked? Was coaching an outlet for my personal desire to compete, and would I feel frustrated if that outlet weren't available? Y-Winners made me step back and ask myself if I would have as much fun without these enticements.

I found that I did. In fact, I had a lot of fun. I toned down my competitive fervor. My daughter loved the program and was eager to play in Y-Winners again.

I think eliminating the scoring was perfectly acceptable to her, and she didn't miss it a bit. She grew as a person and as an athlete, and she felt like a winner at the end of the season, as I'm sure most kids did on most teams.

What would happen if we eliminated scoring in Little League, as we do at the T-ball level? Would it be more fun for the kids if we removed the stigma of losing?

Would parents and coaches behave better, yell less, throw fewer tantrums, and allow referees and umpires to go about their officiating in peace?

I hope you'll have a chance to coach in a nonscoring atmosphere at least once. Then, you'll be able to compare the experiences for yourself. You may find, as I did, that it's hard to let go of certain competitive rituals, but once you do, you may not miss them. You could discover that there are lots of ways to win when you no longer fear losing.

91.
Are You Going to Teach Zen or Dale Carnegie?

WHEN WE EXPERIENCE setbacks, should we buckle down and try harder, or should we emotionally detach ourselves from the bad outcomes?

I call this a Dale-Carnegie-versus-Zen question. As I see it, Carnegie would have us feel the pain of defeat only a moment before pressing onward toward our next victory, whereas Zen would say that winning and losing are illusions, and getting caught up in them, one way or another, is foolish.

When it comes to coaching sports, these attitudes translate into two ways of telling your team to handle defeats. You could say either "We'll beat them the next time!" or "Hey—it's only a game!"

Listen to most coaches and you'll hear both of these sentiments—sometimes in the same speech. But these pronouncements come from very different perspectives. **You should determine what you really believe so that you can be as consistent as possible in communicating a coherent coaching philosophy.**

If you take what I term the Dale Carnegie approach, you're implicitly saying three things to your players:

1. Winning is much better than losing.

2. This loss is a negative event that we need to get over emotionally.

3. The way we'll get over it is by focusing on winning the next game.

This places a burden on your players to win and to keep winning. Otherwise, if they repeatedly lose, they'll probably keep feeling bad about it. Your rhetoric is setting them up to feel high with wins and low with losses.

On the other hand, if you take a Zen approach that "It's only a game," this will put your team into a different frame of mind. Logic suggests that if you admonish them not to get too unhappy with a loss, you might also be saying "Don't become overly jubilant with a win."

In other words, by trying to take the sting out of losses, could you have the effect of making victories less joyful?

After considering these philosophies, you might be tempted to straddle. Why not be Dale Carnegie when your team is winning and a Zen monk when it isn't faring as well? Wouldn't that give you the best of both worlds?

I'd recommend this tactic if I thought it would work, but I think if you alternate from one to another, you'll confuse your players. You could come across as being really bummed out over one defeat while seeming lackadaisical about another.

I believe that we set an important tone for our players largely as a result of how they see us handle adversity. Later in life, long after they've retired from organized sports, they'll confront these issues again and again. Only then, they'll be dealing with career and lifestyle events. How they deal with life's highs and lows may be informed, at least in part, by what you taught them, and whose philosophy you chose to espouse.

92.

It's About More than Having Fun

IF YOU ASK most parents why they're signing their kids up for sports, they'll tell you, "It's just to have fun." That sounds reasonable enough.

Fun is what many folks think childhood should be aimed at—a carefree time in which we're simply allowed to "be." Soon enough, they feel, their kids will be expected to "do."

What these parents don't appreciate is that many kids aren't content to simply be. They want to do, to act, to learn things, and to become increasingly masterful in their worlds. One type of mastery pertains to making their bodies do wonderful things, whether it is running faster, kicking farther, or keeping fly balls from popping out of their gloves.

To become masterful with anything requires focused work. In sports, kids have to work first in order to have fun later.

Just look at what it takes to master the core skills of any sport. First, one's muscles have to be trained because they aren't accustomed to being used in certain ways. If you've hardly ever thrown a softball and suddenly you're expected to do so with a degree of strength and accuracy, you're going to ache after several attempts.

Is the aching fun? Of course not, but it is a phase you'll need to tolerate if you wish to acclimate your body to the rigors of softball and to enjoy the game's rewards.

In addition, one has to work to understand the rules of a sport, and to learn certain strategies for playing in a competitive setting. It's also a form of work to motivate yourself to do your best when you're not feeling well, or after your team has suffered a major loss.

If there's so much work involved in playing sports, you might wonder, when do the kids start having fun?

They have fun when the work no longer seems like work—when they're so interested in the game that they forget they're sweating.

I've heard parents say "I hope the coach doesn't work the kids too hard. We're just here to have fun." Of course, this is naive. If kids, coaches, and parents don't engage in the requisite work, fun won't just happen by itself. To hope it will is like wishing that every meal consisted of only desserts.

Some parents want to prolong their vision of the idyllic childhood— one in which there are no stresses, no boo-boos, no fears, and no expectations. But by the time kids are old enough to speak and to attend school, these perfectionistic wishes should be put aside. Instead, we should hope that our kids will learn to love working, and that they'll come to appreciate, while they're young, that anything worthwhile usually will be achieved only through a substantial expenditure of focused effort.

Yes, we're here to have fun, but this can't be our only objective.

93.

Why Coaches Yell

LOTS OF COACHES are vilified for yelling at their players. Parents hear them and recoil, wondering, "Why can't they pick on someone their own size?"

What are these coaches trying to accomplish when they're yelling? Are they venting frustrations? Are they merely taking shots at their players? Or, are they trying to accomplish a constructive result?

In truth, some coaches do seem loud as well as malicious. I managed in a league with a coach who was verbally abusive. He'd openly mock his pitchers if they were slipping up. He'd say, "Go ahead, Jill. Walk another one. If that's what you want to do, you go right ahead."

When he was disgusted, he didn't conceal it, and I think he crossed the line several times between acceptable and unacceptable criticism of his players. Often, I'd cringe when he'd launch into a tirade.

When I was playing high school baseball, our coach was known to be a curmudgeon. Nearing retirement age, he didn't seem to care what he said or what harm his comments could cause. On a particularly gusty day when I was playing third base, I tried to field a high pop fly but it glanced off my glove, fell to the ground, and allowed the hitter to reach first base.

Between innings, I returned to the dugout, feeling awful. The coach made me feel even worse when he snickered, "Nice catch, butterfingers!" It hurt because I had tried hard to track the ball as it whipsawed in the air.

Unlike the case with these examples, I believe most parent-coaches aren't malicious. They're simply *loud*.

They raise their voices for several understandable reasons. They do it because they're excited. They also shout to get the attention of their players, which seems to wander incessantly. They yell to make sure their outfielders can hear and understand where they should position themselves for left-handed hitters. And they bellow out their encouragment when they cheer their players on.

I don't think most parents have a problem with these sorts of vocalizations. They must realize that a ball field isn't a library, and coaches can't be expected to whisper.

But when the coaches' comments turn negative, they become amplified, if only in the minds of listeners. I suspect that most coaches who are accused of sounding abusive are unaware of how they are coming across to others.

My curmudgeonly high school coach said later that he thought he was being funny by calling me "butterfingers." Looking back on that blustery day, when we were getting beaten by a wide margin, I suppose it would have been better if I had tried to laugh it off and forget about my blooper.

For the most part, coaches who yell during games and who are perceived as being negative are simply trying to correct their players' behavior. Let's say the catcher is allowing balls to pass by him. His coach may yell out, "Block the ball, Billy!" If the coach instead saves this tip for a time when it can be calmly communicated, more balls may go unblocked, and the accumulation of errors could contribute to a loss. Plus, Billy will remain in the habit of not responding appropriately to certain pitches.

Psychologists tell us that feedback should come as quickly as possible after an event, in order to have reinforcement value and thus shape subsequent performances. This suggests that the player who does something well should be immediately praised, while the one who does the opposite should be immediately corrected.

Coaches who actively provide feedback during games are intuitively following this principle. However, they might be better advised, for the purpose of reducing misunderstandings, to save their negative critiques for practices. Practices are more private than games. There's no opposing team, and fewer parents are there, so there is less risk that players will lose face when they're corrected.

I know a number of coaches who say, "You can't really coach during games." By game time, they believe, it's too late to teach anything; you're better off to let events take their course.

But some coaches can't operate in a laid-back way. While they might not be as agitated and verbally abusive as Bobby Knight at Indiana, they can't be wallflowers either.

If you're a "yeller," you probably know it. Remember that you do have a degree of control over it, and you can tone it down. You'll have to if you want to get along in kids' sports.

I think you'll find at this level, the rule is "Loud is bad"—at least in the minds of most parents and many of the players. It doesn't matter that you have a pure heart or that you really know your sport. In this case, communication guru Marshall McLuhan was right: unfortunately, the medium *is* the message.

94.
It's Too Soon to Be Discussing Scholarships

AT FIVE OR six years of age, children start to exhibit some fairly significant athletic differences.

Some have an acute sense of balance. They're able to dribble a soccer ball down the field with relative ease, while their peers move a few feet and either trip over the ball or kick it too hard and have to chase it.

Others have excellent eye-and-hand coordination and can easily hit a softball off a tee. At the same time, their less coordinated buddies are lucky to make contact one in five attempts. You'll also see some naturally athletic kids scoop up ground balls with the sort of finesse that you'd be happy to witness in teenagers.

Inevitably, when one child stands out, parents will talk. "Allie is great, isn't she? She makes it look so easy!"

Before long, this complimentary observation will be transformed into pressure. Allie's parents will be urgently advised by other parents: "You have to keep her in sports. If she plays like this, she'll definitely be able to get an athletic scholarship!"

The wheels will start spinning, like on TV's *Wheel of Fortune*, except the prize in this contest is a completely paid-for college education. I have to admit that this is a pleasant thought. Heck, if my daughter qualifies to attend an expensive school on an athletic scholarship, wouldn't I be a fool to stand in her way?

Sadly, many are called, but few are chosen. The odds are that in any given year, only one or two kids from an entire league can make the cut and be able to play college sports. Even fewer will be economically supported by the institution they choose to attend.

This doesn't prevent parents from talking, only they don't know how counterproductive their patter can be. Allie is a real girl, and the other parents' comments are a direct quote.

She was a wonderful player, both in soccer, where I first met her, and in softball. But just as the "buzz" was spreading about her rosy future, something strange started to happen.

She dropped balls that were thrown to her at first base. During one game alone, I counted errors on six routine plays in a row. She would swing at the air when she was at the plate. Still in T-ball, this meant something was wrong with her, and not with the pitchers, because there weren't any.

To this day, Allie hasn't regained her coordination or natural grace on the playing field. Oddly, she seems happier than she was when she was a standout.

Making errors could have been her nonverbal way of reducing the pressures of her parents' soaring aspirations. By regressing, she could be treated as just another player and not have to perform like a "scholarship baby."

As coaches, we should be careful about what we say to kids or to their parents about playing abilities. It's OK to be encouraging, but we shouldn't take the joy out of letting players, gifted or average, develop at their own pace.

95.
What Should We Be Teaching Through Sports?

ASK PARENTS WHAT they hope their children will get from the organized sports experience and you can hear more than two dozen different answers. They include:

1. Sportsmanship

2. Leadership

3. Teamwork

4. A positive mental attitude

5. Self-esteem

6. Self-confidence

7. Loyalty

8. Commitment

9. Social skills

10. Friendship

11. Competitive abilities

12. A "winner's mentality"

13. Fortitude

14. Discipline

15. The ability to follow directions

16. A sense of accomplishment

17. Coordination

18. Exercise

19. Strength

20. Knowledge of the game

21. A connection with the parent's childhood

22. Resiliency

23. Hardiness

24. Fun

25. A pleasant overall experience

This is quite a wish list, isn't it?

I'd like you to try an experiment: rank these twenty-five "values" in their order of importance to you. If you find the task too daunting, at least rank your top five and bottom five. I think you'll find this exercise to be an eye-opener.

When I taught at the college level, I'd have my classes do this sort of task as a way of grasping what their values are. After discovering them, they could make inferences about other people's values and thereby craft better communications for different constituencies.

For a prospective coach, it's important to "know thy values" before you sign on to run a team. By the same token, it's helpful to postulate what the values of your team's parents and players happen to be. My hunch is that most of your conflicts will arise from the differences you have in the sports values you embrace.

For example, I would probably list the following as my top five values:

1. Ability to follow directions

2. Knowledge of the game

3. Commitment

4. Positive mental attitude

5. Coordination

Here's why I emphasize these. First, if you can't get your team to follow basic directions, you'll face chaos at every practice and game.

Second, kids need to know enough of the rules pertaining to the game to know what is and isn't permissible.

Third, they need to foster a commitment to learning and to growing. Minimally, they have to show up for most of the events and to arrive and depart on time.

Fourth, it's essential to have a positive, can-do mentality. If they don't bring it with them at the season's start, they should definitely leave with it.

Fifth, they need to have minimal coordination to make the moves and to complete the mechanics that any activity requires.

If they bring the first four to the task, I believe coordination will be learned and improved. I suppose, if I had to capture the essence of the first five values in a single statement, it would be: Kids need to have a desire to learn, they need to pay attention, and then they need to try to physicalize what they have learned.

If these values are in place, a number of other results will naturally flow from them. They'll see that they're making progress, and this recognition will contribute to feelings of self-esteem, self-confidence, and a sense of accomplishment.

(By the way, my sixth value would be a winner's mentality. As long as we're scoring contests, and winners are distinguished from losers, kids need to know that making up their minds to be victorious is part of the game.)

My bottom five would be ranked this way:

21. Connection with the parent's childhood

22. Friendship

23. Social skills

24. Fun

25. Pleasant overall experience

I think these are fine results, but they are natural by-products of playing the game. I don't think you have to "try" to produce these outcomes, and if you are trying, you're not focusing on the more important dynamics of the sport.

I don't expect you to agree with my rankings, but that's my point. We should expect to disagree, and by ranking what we feel is really important, we can start an intelligent dialogue. Coaches can clearly identify what they cherish, and if they're not on the same page as the parents or the league, they can reconsider their decision to coach.

Likewise, parents who might self-righteously feel at odds with someone's coaching style may be able to use a checklist like this to determine why they're in disagreement.

In any case, we could be teaching any number of things through kids' sports. I think we'll do a lot better if we know what we can choose from. Then we can select the essential items and allow the rest to naturally follow.

96.
Should Players Be Redrafted Each Year?

IT IS A long-standing tradition in most municipal baseball leagues that once players are selected by a team, they'll stay on that team for the entire time they're playing in that division.

In Little Leagues where players are eligible from ages nine through twelve, a nine-year-old will play with the same team for all four years. I used to think this was a perfectly suitable arrangement, until I became a parent, and then a coach in the American Youth Soccer Organization.

AYSO forms new teams at the beginning of each season and dissolves them just as quickly when the season concludes. This has numerous advantages:

1. It makes kids friendly competitors. Knowing that next year or the year after, they may be teammates of this year's opponents, players don't become as destructively competitive as they could otherwise be. Also, there isn't any time to create team-versus-team rivalries which can degenerate into feuds. Depending on the size of the league, teams may end up facing each other only once—unless they make it to the play-offs.

2. Parents who may dislike a particular coach won't have the same motivation to agitate against the leader if they know that the team will endure for only a matter of weeks, and not years. It's easier to let bygones be bygones in a temporary atmosphere.

3. Players make more friends by changing teams. This is especially helpful to those who don't have siblings because they can develop a larger pool of playmates from which to draw for off-the-field fun.

4. Parents get to know more parents, which deepens their associations as well as connections to the community.

5. It helps to distribute playing talent equally. Redrafting every season means that coaches can "rate" players more frequently and thus can take into account sudden surges in playing ability. And "powerhouse" teams don't grow into unbeatable dynasties when players are redistributed every year.

6. Coaches and managers also have single-season commitments. This reduces the pressure on them to perform and to please. If they have a positive experience, they volunteer to coach again. If not, they're only weeks away from a graceful retirement.

7. Kids are exposed to more coaches, and to different leadership philosophies and communication styles. They're therefore more likely to develop a positive relationship with one of them, which will enhance their attitude toward sports. By seeing more parents taking part, they'll implicitly perceive that *they* can contribute to their own kids' teams later in life.

8. Shuffling the deck more often increases kids' chances of playing a variety of positions. They're seen as new resources each season, and coaches will try them at various spots on their teams.

Ayso soccer is relatively new among sports leagues. Therefore, it can rethink traditional approaches to the formation and coaching of teams. I think it has made a smart move in choosing to redraft players each year. We should consider applying the same principle to more established sports leagues.

97.
Choose a Value, and
Then Teach It!

THE Y-WINNERS basketball program is notable in a number of respects, and it contains some important lessons for sports parents. One I learned in a class for new coaches in which our trainer stressed, "Choose a value for the kids, and then teach it!"

What did he mean? And why is it so important?

Most of us presume that certain values will be transmitted to our kids simply by their participating in league sports. For instance, we assume that they'll learn to play by the rules, that they'll respect their fellow players and coaches, and that they'll learn about the importance of teamwork.

But this type of knowledge doesn't just happen by playing. Most of their attention will be directed to learning and then refining athletic mechanics. In basketball, kids will learn to dribble, pass, shoot, and guard. In baseball, they'll run, catch, throw, and hit. In soccer, they'll pay attention to kicking and positioning themselves to make and receive passes.

Much of our coaching will be invested in drills that attempt to make these physical moves as reflexive as possible. This type of activity can be a lot of fun for kids because each sport has a certain rhythm that clicks in when the mechanics are performed smoothly. So, they're not going to object if we forget about instilling values. More's the pity, because they won't realize what they're missing.

In the Y-Winners program, I was one of three coaches on our team. At our first practice, our head coach, Phil Van Horn, stated what he felt were important objectives. He told the players, "This season we have three goals: to have fun, to make friends, and to play fairly."

Our team consisted of girls in grades first through third. So, they ranged from six to nine years old. Despite their relative immaturity, each child, even the youngest, immediately understood that we had a direction.

Phil asked them to repeat his trilogy aloud. Like a chorus, they intoned, "We're going to have fun, make friends, and play fairly!"

This mantra was repeated often during the course of our season. We'd always ask the players, "Are you having fun?"

To assist them to bond and to make new friends, we also asked the girls to state the names of at least two other players on the team. Before long, everyone was on a first-name basis, and we took on an essential feeling of unity.

Of course, we taught the specifics of what we considered to be "fair" practices. These included sharing the ball by passing, being willing to come out of a game to give another person time to play, and trying to show up to practices on time so that we could smoothly develop our skills as a team.

Sometimes, after a scrimmage or a game, one of our players would comment about the opposition, "They didn't play fairly!" Our kids knew that this was a violation of what we believed in as a team.

As the end of the season came upon us, our head coach again asked the players what our goals were. They repeated them in order—and with feeling! Equally important was the fact that the recurring recitation of these values kept us focused as coaches while also informing parents about what we were really endorsing.

So, choose a value and teach it!

98.
Remember to Coach One Game at a Time

MARK McGWIRE, WHILE having his record-setting, seventy-home-run season, paused to have a photograph taken with his dad, his college coach from USC, and his Little League coach. It was a scene that would warm any coach's heart.

It must feel great to be credited with helping to develop the abilities of a future Hall of Famer, but this fantasy shouldn't become even a remote objective as we take the reins of a kids' team. While an extremely small percentage of our youngsters will make their way into the athletic big time, if we gear our coaching to producing these superstars, we'll be making a major mistake.

There are a number of little things that coaches tend to do when they feel they have a potential superstar on their team, the worst of which is to rely on that player far too much to carry the rest of the group. Here again, I speak from experience.

I was an assistant coach on a soccer team that had two tall girls on the roster. They were literally head and shoulders above their peers in appearance as well as athletic ability. Everyone could see this in a heartbeat, including the other kids on the team.

Along with the other coaches and most of the players, I expected this pair to be great. Without realizing it at the time, we began to defer to them. Instead of aggressively going for the ball, our smaller kids would wait to see if one of the bigger kids would kick it first.

When our star players had to attend Girl Scout functions or miss games for other reasons, it ended up causing big problems. Our more average players didn't have the confidence to step up and carry the team by themselves. In fact, they had become convinced that they couldn't win without our big guns in the lineup.

It took an effort to overcome this belief and to empower the rest of the team, but we did it before all was lost.

In the process, we learned an important lesson. Instead of concerning ourselves with the potential careers of our superstars, we should have been paying more attention to the rest of the team. And instead of coaching for tomorrow or for the record books, we should have been coaching just one game at a time.

PART XII

Parting
Thoughts

99.
How to Tell Your Kids You're *Not* Coaching

IF YOU THINK coaching is difficult, try to explain to your kid that you're going to retire from this "hobby."

After you have coached for a few seasons, or have managed a few different sports, your child will expect to see you in a leadership position. If you recede into the bleachers and become just another parent, the child can feel somewhat disoriented, if not crestfallen.

I decided to hang up my spikes one season, and I thought my daughter would be absolutely delighted. I figured she'd be thrilled to get 100 percent of Papa's attention. Finally, I could help her in every aspect of her sport.

If she needed hitting practice, we could make our own exclusive pilgrimage to the batting cage. She wouldn't have to contend with Dad's habit of putting other players ahead of her in the interest of seeming fair and objective.

We could return to the biased bliss in which parents and their offspring dwell. Heck, we could become a real family again!

All of these expectations were dashed when my baby asked, "Dad— why aren't you coaching?"

I couldn't believe my ears. "You *miss* my coaching?"

"Yeah, Dad. You're the best. You're a lot better than Sid."

She had to be kidding. I thought she loved Sid, in that way that kids have of developing a crush on their friends' parents. So, why was I suddenly being missed so much?

I could see the answer written on her face. As long as I was the Number One Dad, the Coach, Head Honcho, and all of that, my special status flowed to her as well. She could be a minor celebrity. OK—maybe not that special—but she was treated with respect, and the best players on the field paid attention to her.

She was in a special class. She belonged to that club whose members are the families that move and shake the league.

She was telling me she was going to miss that. I suppose she never appreciated her special stature when coaching was the normal role for her dad. But now that my intense demeanor was slipping into memory, a certain intimacy was leaving the sport for her.

Now she would have to play because *she* wanted to and not because her family was committed to it. That meant she needed to ask herself "Do I really want to continue with this if the pressure of being a coach's kid is no longer on my shoulders?"

I'm happy to say that my daughter's answer was "Yes!" She loves sports, whether I'm calling the shots or not. She wants to be out there with her buddies.

Every now and then, you should consider giving the sport back to the kids, by retiring from coaching. It's one of the few ways we have of discovering whether they're really playing for themselves or, secretly, for us.

100.

You've Gotta Believe in Miracles

"Coach, I'm going to hit this one out for you . . ."

This is what one of my players whispered in my ear while I was standing in the third-base coaching box. She had been having a wondrous day already. She pitched four great innings, hit two homers, and drove in most of our runs. Despite the fact that we were way ahead on the scoreboard, my little champion wasn't through.

"I'm going to hit this one out for you . . ."

Could she do it? Legend has it that the great Babe Ruth "called his shot" before hitting a historic homer into dead center field. He said he'd do it, and he did it.

My ace player was looking me straight in the eye. Would the cosmic forces let her pull it off? Did she even have the strength left in her body to blast the ball after having pitched so hard?

On a two-and-one count, the answer was heard throughout the park. She belted a long drive to left. It was like the movie in which angels lift a player's feet off the field and scoot him or her around the bases.

The two outfielders closest to the ball gave chase and caught up with it just as my player rounded second. The left fielder, who was big and strong, bare-handed it, wheeled around, and rocketed it back toward the infield. This play was going to be *close*!

I started circling my left arm—the signal to keep running. "Score! Score! Score!" I yelled.

Nothing could stop her—I could see that. She was going to do something that she'd remember for the rest of her life. The crowd went nuts when she slid into home. Safely!

She was in the "zone" that day. This is a frame of mind in which you do everything well—effortlessly. It has been described as being like a state of grace. It can happen in any human endeavor, but it's especially wonderful when it occurs in sports because other people can see it and share in it.

It's the sports equivalent of being blessed by a miracle. I hope that you'll be able to witness at least one as a coach. If you do, you'll never forget it.

101.

Is It All Worth It?

You've come a long way in this book, and I want to thank you for persevering. As you know, this is my final observation. As the title promised, it's the 101st.

It's my short answer to the fundamental question you have probably asked yourself about coaching kids' sports: Is it worth it?

To this point, you've seen that coaching can involve numerous pitfalls, many of which you probably never anticipated. It's time consuming, it's physically demanding, and it can jeopardize your peace of mind.

Kids will show up late for games and then complain when you don't immediately pull a player out to insert them in the lineup. You may find yourself dealing with obnoxious and potentially violent coaches, referees, and fans.

People will say mean things, and despite the fact that you're a fairly mild-mannered person, you'll find that you're quite capable of yelling. Parents will want the sporting experience to shape their children in any number of ways, and occasionally their philosophies will clash with yours.

League officials will seem like village idiots who are never there when you need them and all over you like a swarm of killer bees when you don't.

You'll wonder why it's so *hard* to be a volunteer. On a number of occasions, you'll ask yourself, "Why am I putting more effort into coaching this team than I'm putting into my career?"

When your team loses, you'll mentally replay the errors they made, insisting that if one or two plays had gone differently, you would have won. You'll calculate and recalculate exactly how many games you'll need to win in order to get into the play-offs.

Occasionally, you'll find yourself sailing on a cloud of euphoria because your players came through in the clutch and won in the last few minutes of a tough contest. And you'll grieve and blame yourself when your team can't seem to do anything right.

But then, when you're feeling the lowest, you'll remember how your spirit soared the first time a player called you "Coach." You'll see that your child walks just a little bit taller because you're totally involved with the team.

You'll make scores of mistakes, mostly out of inexperience. Then, when you finally get the knack of coaching, your kid will "graduate" to a higher league in which your services will no longer be required.

You'll look at the familiar team photograph, where you're standing like a statue at the side of your players. And you'll realize: It's better to have coached and lost than never to have coached at all.

Is it worth it? You bet it is.

I highly recommend it as one of the most interesting ways to connect your inner child to the real child you're raising. Plus, it's one of the few ways you can find a bunch of people who will be willing to play your favorite sport with you!

So, jump in there, and good luck!

Afterword

THANK YOU FOR reading this book. I hope you got as much out of it as I did!

Writing it helped me to come to terms with the same issues that you'll be facing as a volunteer coach. It also gave me some closure and a feeling of accomplishment.

But enough about me!

When I'm not coaching, I am a communication consultant to companies and small businesses, so I thrive on feedback. Did you like this book? Would you recommend it to other people? If I were to write another one on this topic, what should I include next time? Do you have any great stories to share or plain-old questions? Please let me know.

Best of luck to you!

Gary S. Goodman, Ph.D.
P.O. Box 9733
Glendale, CA 91226-9733
Voice: (818) 243-7338
Fax: (818) 956-2242
E-mail: goodmanorg@earthlink.net

Index